A HISTORY

of

PACIFIC NORTHWEST CUISINE

MASTODONS TO MOLECULAR GASTRONOMY

MARC HINTON

EDITED BY PAMELA HEILIGENTHAL

AMERICAN PALATE

Published by American Palate
A Division of The History Press
Charleston, SC 29403
www.historypress.net

Front cover, top: Red grapes. *Courtesy Pamela Heiligenthal; bottom left*: Landscape and covered wagon. *Courtesy Bob Wick, Bureau of Land Management; bottom right*: Tomatoes. *Courtesy Pamela Heiligenthal.*

First published 2013

Manufactured in the United States

ISBN 978.1.60949.616.6

Library of Congress CIP data applied for.

Notice: The information in this book is true and complete to the best of our knowledge. It is offered without guarantee on the part of the author or The History Press. The author and The History Press disclaim all liability in connection with the use of this book.

Contents

Prologue

A s a self-proclaimed culinarian, it is only natural that after spending most of my life devoted to learning about food and wine and living in the Pacific Northwest, I expand my knowledge by seeking out the origins and historical facts relating to the beginning of the foodways of this region. This story will unravel a lot of the mysteries regarding how the inhabitants of the Northwest fed themselves and the techniques and ingredients they used as they progressed from the earliest-known cultures to present day. To understand the whole picture, it is just as important to understand the usage and expansion of indigenous staples and the strong effort to conserve some of the dwindling supplies of unique species of plants, sea life and animals that are near extinction. As I embark on this journey, I would like to bring you along as we discover how the foods of the Northwest nourished the first settlers of this bountiful geographical location for thousands of years.

From my earliest days as a line cook in Boston, I was continually looking for the best ingredients available for my culinary creations and accepted that seasons would dictate the quality and abundance of product sources. When I made my first geographical move to further my career, I migrated to Chicago, where my protein sources expanded but my fresh vegetable and seafood selections dwindled, as did the demand for a broad selection of seafood and produce that were must-haves for menus on the Northeast Coast restaurant scene. Just about the time I had mastered the tastes of the midwestern palate, I made another move that would alter my perception of food products and change my style of cooking forever.

During my first tryout at the Kimpton Group property with Chef John Sedlar's Abiquiu opening, it was obvious my move to San Francisco had revealed a new reality that I had only previously read about; the success of Chef Alice Waters at Chez Panisse was the driving force behind my western migration in the early 1990s. Upon arrival in the San Francisco Bay area, I completed auditions with Joyce Goldstein at Square One and Jeremiah Tower of Stars, and both restaurants offered me positions. I had to pass up both opportunities due to the limited potential of advancement. Instead, I opted for a position with the Kimpton Group because of the rapid expansion and the possibility of upward mobility.

The plan worked as I started with a chef di parti position and worked my way up to executive chef in two short years. I based my decision primarily on the amount of knowledge to be absorbed from the talented staff surrounding me at the Kimpton Group. At no other place in the world at that time would I have had such a vast amount of knowledge to glean from mentors such as Chef Thom Fox, Chef Julian Serrano, Chef Chris Majer, Chef Bob Helstrom and Chef Rob Pando.

On my very first night at the Kimpton Group, I knew I had reached a level of culinary nirvana very few individuals would experience. In early May, we had heirloom tomatoes to offer our guests in a composed salad of tomato, baby lettuces and fresh goat cheese formed into marbles, mounted on fresh rosemary spears and rolled in a mixture of roasted nuts and finely chopped fresh herbs. The accompanying vinaigrette did not compete for attention and paired well with wine. As much as I knew I had crossed over into uncharted territory, I did not know how unlimited the quality of fresh vegetables and artisan raised livestock had changed now that I was on the West Coast.

It would be a couple years before culinary nirvana would rock my world again during a Kimpton Group Executive Chef and General Manager retreat. That year, they held the event in Puget Sound, and my world was turned upside down when I took my first tour of Pike Place Market, where I was exposed to the bounty of Northwest produce and seafood. It was a glorious sight. I was immediately convinced that the availability of products in the Northwest far surpassed the quality and selection I was working with in California. The possibilities of what could be created with these raw products were quickly brought into focus when we ate with Chef Tom Douglas at Etta's followed by some memorable meals prepared by Chef Walter Pisano of Tulio's and Chef Tim Kelley of the Painted Table. This Seattle excursion also afforded me a first glimpse of a serious wine program when I enjoyed a meal at Thai Ginger, an Asian restaurant concept. I then spent some time in the Olympic Peninsula exploring Port Townsend and even foraging for local mushrooms.

Upon leaving the Seattle area, I arrived back in San Francisco with a newfound creative drive that was largely inspired by the revelations discovered on that retreat. Combining my knowledge of regional Italian fare and unusual Northwest produce and seafood, we generated sales at the newly opened Puccini & Pinetti that surprised even the hotel's and restaurant operations's vice-presidents, Steve Puccini and Bob Pinetti. It was at this point in my culinary career that a small accident would change my life forever and dictate how active I could be in a kitchen. A fall while running down a flight of stairs resulted in the destruction of my right elbow. This event set the stage for my crossover to working the front of the house in restaurants and eventually my introduction to working at wineries. At first, I went from running the back of the house in restaurants to the front of the house while consulting on new concepts and building wine lists for popular new ventures, working first in the Northern California wine industry and then moving south to Paso Robles on the Central Coast.

In 1999, a small twist of fate brought Pamela, my loving wife and partner for twenty-five years, and I to Seattle for a wine expo held by the Italian Trade Commission. This visit would be Pamela's first trip to the Northwest, and it had the same profound effect on her as it did for me on my first visit. The Italian wine expo was a huge success, and our exploration of Puget Sound brought a myriad of reasons to move to this alluring region, especially with its proximity to one of the most beautiful cities in the world, Vancouver, British Columbia. No sooner than we had started our drive back to central California did we begin discussing the possibility of relocating to the Northwest.

One factor that figured prominently in making the decision to pull up stakes in Paso Robles was the detour off Interstate 5 to Highway 99, which led us to Dundee, where we would visit our first Oregon winery. As we passed through the city of Newberg, I recognized the city's name as one I had seen on a few bottles of Oregon Pinot noir. Although there are quite a few tasting rooms on Highway 99 now, there were only a few back in 1999. When I saw the Argyle sign on the left hand side of the highway, I recognized it as one of the well-known Oregon wineries. I had tasted Argyle's products previously and was impressed at first sip, especially with their sparkling wines and Pinot noir. The tasting room experience was fun and educational, but most of all, it was different. Projecting a gracious warmth of hospitality, our tasting room host framed the experience in a way that set it apart from other wine regions I had visited in the past.

As we departed Argyle's tasting room, my mind started to drift toward all I had experienced in Washington and Oregon, leading me to ponder the origins of this unique culture, especially how it had flourished in locations that remained unchanged for at least ten millennia after the first inhabitants arrived.

Over a decade later, I attempt to offer a chronological account of events that focuses on how the Northwest lifestyle has developed into one of the hottest food and wine movements happening in the world right now. Most importantly, I would like to point out the food was always here, but it took a while for the wines to catch up.

Chapter One

Man Eats Mastodon and Is Still Hungry

A good place to start with this journey is the Happy Valley archaeological dig, which took place in Sequim, Washington. On a sunny August afternoon in 1977, bowling alley owner Emanuel "Manny" Manis decided he wanted a pond in his front yard. Manny and his wife, Clare, had moved to the sleepy retirement community a few years earlier to quietly live out their lives and live off the land, practicing the quintessential Northwest pioneer lifestyle of existing self-sufficiently in the house they built with their own hands. On this particular afternoon, Manny went out and cranked up his backhoe to excavate a hole in his front yard in the typical Northwest do-it-yourself style to create a water view. He was not digging long before he hit what he thought were two old mud-covered logs measuring four to six inches in diameter and four to six feet long.

Manny, being quite surprised at having found what looked like two elephant tusks buried in his front yard, yelled for his wife to witness what he had dug up. Clare begrudgingly came down to see what the hell her crazy husband was talking about. Admittedly being quite skeptical, she quickly realized that they were actual tusks and decided to call around to see if anyone was interested in the discovery. What was about to unravel was the beginning of the Pacific Northwest's account of its earliest human foodways.

After a week or so and several attempts at finding someone who might care about the discovery, Clare stumbled on anthropologist Dr. Richard Daugherty and archaeologist-zoologist Dr. Carl Gustafson, both of Washington State

Mastodon bones from the Manis Mastodon site, which are on display at the Museum & Arts Center (MAC) exhibition in Sequim, Washington. *Courtesy of Pamela Heiligenthal.*

Sitting just off the road where an archaeological dig took place, a concrete monument sits firmly where Emanuel "Manny" Manis discovered the mastodon bones in August 1977, linking man and mastodon for the first time on the North American continent. *Courtesy of Pamela Heiligenthal.*

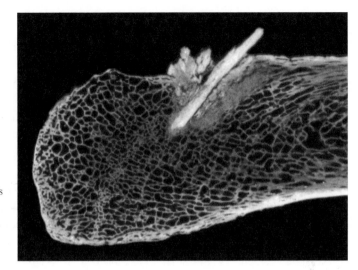

High-tech CT scans show the point embedded in the mammoth's rib bone. *Courtesy Center for the Study of the First Americans, Texas A&M University.*

University. Once Gustafson heard of the discovery, he immediately grabbed an eight-foot-long roll of cotton batting and a two-and-a-half-ton truck and descended to the site with Daugherty on August 17, 1977. Upon arrival, the two professors quickly realized this was something they could hang their hats on. Gustafson initially thought he would be there for a short time, but as it turned out, he would return every summer until 1985.

This archaeological dig represents the earliest confirmed discovery of human inhabitants on the Pacific Coast south of Alaska. According to the Center for the Study of the First Americans, many researchers disputed the age of this find until 2011, when new technology confirmed the date of the tusks to be 13,800 years old. What makes this finding particularly interesting is that Gustafson discovered a bone projectile point embedded in the rib bone of the mastodon, which marks the earliest date humans appear to have been feeding themselves on the Pacific Coast.

One aspect that puzzled some was that initially, only one-half of the mastodon was found. Then, as Gustafson looked around, he realized that the half of the mastodon they discovered came from a location that was at a much lower elevation than the geographical topography that surrounded the site. In fact, the mastodon did not die from the sharpened killing tool that was imbedded in the animal but from a later attack. They found the other half of the mastodon not too far away. The half found on higher ground had been butchered, thus confirming our native northwestern ancestors ate meat almost fourteen millennia ago near the most northwestern point of what is now the United States.

I doubt that when Manny Manis dreamed of putting a pond in his front yard, he would have ever imagined the story unfolding the way it did. This event predates the previously held notion that the Clovis people were the first to make the Bering Strait land bridge crossing by foot traveling from Siberia to Alaska and down the Pacific Coast. This hypothesis is supported by the Paisley Caves excavation site in Oregon near Bend. Further evidence supports a pre-Clovis occupation of the New World, according to Fagundes, et al., in the *American Journal of Human Genetics*, which states:

> *Here we show, by using 86 complete mitochondrial genomes, that all Native American haplogroups, including haplogroup X, were part of a single founding population, thereby refuting multiple-migration models. A detailed demographic history of the mtDNA sequences estimated with a Bayesian coalescent method indicates a complex model for the peopling of the Americas, in which the initial differentiation from Asian populations ended with a moderate bottleneck in Beringia during the last glacial maximum (LGM), around Ð23,000 to Ð19,000 years ago. Toward the end of the LGM, a strong population expansion started Ð18,000 and finished Ð15,000 years ago. These results support a pre-Clovis occupation of the New World, suggesting a rapid settlement of the continent along a Pacific coastal route.*

The Ecological Impacts That Led to the Extinction of Megafaunal Species

The existence of the mastodon bone in Carl Gustafson's site points to one of the earliest staples of the Paleo-Indian diet, along with deer, bison, horse and camel. Yes, there were camels in North America at one time, as well as quite a few other large mammals, which are now extinct. A well-known mass extinction of megafauna occurred at the end of the last ice age, which wiped out many of the giant ice age animals in America. A number of theories exist, alternatively attributing this extinction to climate change, human hunting, disease or other causes, such as the Younger Dryas impact or Clovis comet hypothesis. A definitive explanation is yet to be discovered as new speculations, such as the methane gas theory, have been hypothesized. Nowadays, even the mention of methane gas will usually cause folks to chuckle, but it really is serious business in this context. Correspondence published in 2010 from the journal *Nature Geoscience* states that herbivores produce methane as a byproduct of foregut fermentation in digestion and release it through belching. Large populations of herbivore megafauna have a high potential to contribute greatly to the atmospheric concentration of methane. Even today, roughly 20 percent of annual methane emissions come from livestock. Recent studies indicate that the extinction of megafaunal herbivores may have caused a reduction in atmospheric methane, but this hypothesis is relatively new. Yet another study examined the change of methane concentration in the atmosphere at the end of the Pleistocene epoch after the extinction of megafauna in the Americas:

> *After early humans migrated to the Americas ~13,000 BP* [before the present], *their hunting and other ecological impacts led to the extinction of many megafaunal species. Calculations suggest extinction decreased methane production by ~9.6 Tg/yr* [teragrams per year]. *Ice core records support this hypothesis of rapid methane decrease during the period. This suggests that the absence of megafaunal methane emissions may have contributed to the abrupt climatic cooling at the onset of the Younger Dryas.*

IF IT FLIES OR SWIMS, YOU CAN PROBABLY EAT IT

Before cross-contamination from the interaction with western man, Paleo-Indian diets were limited to just a few indigenous food sources. The Paleo diet (short for Paleolithic) references to an era before agriculture took hold. During this time, our diets consisted of meats, nuts and gathered wild vegetables and fresh fruits. Most importantly, it did not include grains, salt, sugar, legumes or dairy products. Animals were not domesticated, and agriculture was not yet necessary. If you were one of the settlers along the Pacific Coast or an inhabitant of the Channel Islands, your diet would have been different from that of the populations living inland.

The Arlington Springs archaeological site afforded researchers a look at exactly what these people ate, and what the archaeologists discovered was a change in the style of tools used to obtain food and a change in the menu. The excavations on California's northern Channel Islands indicate that these early Americans were seafaring travelers adept at hunting birds and seals, in addition to catching great quantities of fish and shellfish. Their tool-making style, especially the finely worked crescent-shaped blades found by the dozens, connects them to the first people in Oregon, Washington and

Idaho. Artifacts such as delicate barbed projectile points resemble stone tools found in ice age sites as far away as Japan.

In January 2007, the Center for the Study of the First Americans Department of Anthropology at Texas A&M University published a great story in its monthly magazine, *The Mammoth Trumpet*, about what Paleo-Indian diets included when wild game became scarce. The article, "First American Roots—Literally," is very aptly titled. The story revolves around the camas bulb, an inedible plant by most civilizations' standards. Cooking these wonders of the American Northwest takes a painstaking method of processing. In this publication, anthropology professor Dr. Alston Thoms shows how to prepare the camas bulbs in the traditional method used by the Kalispel Indians of Washington State. If steamed for twenty-four to forty-eight hours, these bulbs turn from an inedible plant into the vegetable jerky of that time. Once properly steamed, they would last for ten to twenty years.

Thoms found that camas was a staple in parts of the Pacific Northwest through the Holocene period. The roots could be procured and processed in large quantities. After being cooked in an earth oven, they could be stored for decades. The earth oven partially dehydrated them, and a thin sugary layer coated every surface of the bulb, including any punctures, working as a natural preservative. Thoms recalls the memoirs of David Thompson, mapmaker and explorer of the late 1700s and early 1800s, who wrote of eating cooked camas he had stored for thirty years. Thoms himself can attest to the bulbs' edibility ten years after cooking. Processed camas was the canned food of the archaic period in various parts of North America, from British Columbia to Texas.

Many archaeological sites dating to 9000 RCYBP (radio carbon years before the present) have fire-cracked rocks, indicators of earth ovens. These ovens show that when the Paleo-Indians needed a new way to cook something—in this case, a way to slowly braise camus bulbs for a long period of time—they adapted and built a new tool.

According to Thoms, "Pieces of fire-cracked rock are not nearly as exciting to most archaeologists as say, a Clovis point or a mammoth tusk." OK, so maybe fire cracked rocks aren't very sexy. Nevertheless, archaeologists have known for a century that the sudden appearance in the archaeological record of large ovens filled with fire-cracked rock had something to do with changes in the way people ate or in the way they cooked their food. Dr. Thoms proposes that this evident change, which appears quite pronounced, fits perfectly with evolutionary science of today from the standpoint of both cultural and physical adaptability of humans to changing conditions. Even today, the diet of our ancestors has become a desired weight-loss method—

many new books and articles have been written about the Paleolithic diet and are championed as the new "Atkins diet."

Humans had been living in North America for thousands of years apparently doing perfectly well on diets consisting largely of meat, fish and fowl, but presumably supplemented by vegetables cooked over an open fire.

During this time, monumental changes happened in how people ate. People all over the country began building large earth ovens and cooking root foods. It's perplexing, since almost no evidence of this cooking technology is seen beforehand on this continent. It was a sudden revolution that radically changed eating habits.

Thoms, finding that this sudden upsurge in earth-oven cookery occurred over large areas at essentially the same time, began to look for a common thread. "Some of these areas are deserts," he notes, "some are Pacific maritime forests; some are the Great Plains, and here in Texas and California [they are] in savannah settings." So people inhabiting every type of climate condition except the Arctic suddenly started eating in a different manner. What seems to run common in all of these places at about the same time is that the landscape could no longer support hunting alone due to the overpopulation of humans. Thoms calls the archaic culture's response to this overcrowding as, "land use intensification." He cites Lewis Binford, who says that people in times of privation "will move to smaller game, then to aquatic resources and then to root foods." The considerable time and effort required to process camas bulbs seems to support Thoms's conclusion that something must have compelled people to adopt this more difficult method of cooking.

Is it possible that this technology already existed and humans did not use it because it was not required for subsistence? It makes sense that an increase in population could force people with limited resources to reach back into the past to utilize knowledge of alternative methods of subsistence. The oldest earth ovens, in Japan, date back to 32,000 RCYBP. From here, evolution would be the operating concept that propelled the civilization creating the culture that Western man would encounter when he initially interacted with the First Nations Peoples.

HOW DID THEY GET HERE?

The rapid population expansion on the West Coast seems to lend credence to the theory that there were a couple of different routes migrating people utilized after reaching Alaska. Many researchers have studied at length the rapid expansion of people through the central part of North America because the expansion of population made such a profound effect on many aspects of those peoples' cultures. One aspect of research focuses on what paths the migration routes would have had to follow to facilitate the quick expansion of populations. From Alaska, it is hypothesized that there were three main routes.

The Pacific Coast route by foot and the exposed continental shelf by small boats are theorized to be the most likely routes Pre-Clovis people would have taken. The small boat concept is plausible due to the Channel Island archaeological finds. Only six miles off the coast of California's mainland (now separated by water-covered lowlands), the Channel Islands were inhabited 11,000 years ago. Prior to Carl Gustafson's Happy Valley site in Sequim, the earliest North American inhabitant was thought to have been the bones of a woman, found in 1959, on Santa Rosa, one of the Channel Islands. There is a very enlightening in-depth article about America's First Lady written by the Center for the Study of the First Americans Department of Anthropology.

Prior to confirming the age of the Sequim site (which is 13,800 years old), Arlington Springs (on Santa Rosa Island) was considered the discovery of the first North American inhabitants. The stone tools found at the Arlington site were similar to tools found in Japan from the same period. These artifacts reflect a change in some of the dietary staples of the island inhabitants. On their menu were birds of the sea, seals and sardines. These findings come from shell fragments and bones more than 11,000 years old left behind from meals. This finding gives us a better insight into what the first Americans ate. Through the discovery of these stone tools, we can link people from the Channel Islands to populations living a great distance away. These findings demonstrate the evolution of changing subsistence patterns and how slowly or quickly they are altered to adapt to the needs of civilization as our environment dictates.

In the next chapter, I will visit some historical theories and concepts that deserve notice. Of note, I will talk about the recorded oral histories from tribes, as they existed on this continent underground before finding a hole that led them to a life of living above ground. Additionally, I will talk about a Buddhist priest who arrived on our shores around AD 500 named Hui Shen (慧深), who called North America "Fusang" (扶桑). The reference appears frequently on ancient maps from China. After viewing the maps, it might make you rethink the accepted belief of who the first people from

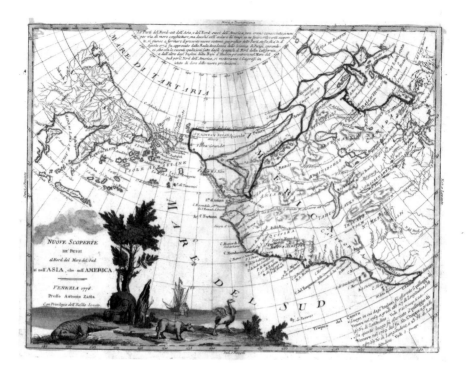

A 1776 Zatta Map of California and the Western Parts of North America by Barry Lawrence Ruderman. *Source provided by Geographicus Rare Antique Maps.*

another culture to visit our shores were. Many of the indigenous peoples on our West Coast were in possession of metal utensils, as noted in many of the written historical accounts of the Spaniards, Britons and Americans. The assumption was that the metal was of Asian origin and had washed up on the beaches of the Northwest from shipwrecks. Metallurgy was common in Asia long before it was prevalent in North America.

With any cultural interaction, there is always some intertwining of food and culinary procedures. As these procedures evolve, they showcase the single greatest thing about getting to know people who are different from you: when cultures collide, they always gain the knowledge of different foods and the techniques to prepare them. As a culinarian working with different cultures, I can attest from my own personal experience this theory has always held true.

Cross-cultural contamination of the first Northwest human inhabitants brought with it many changes. Some were outright atrocities. Some changed the natural evolution of these people forever. Sadly, it would take several hundred years before Western man would realize how much these peoples' traditions would influence the cultures of those who interacted with them. Telling a full history of their early subsistence from scattered sources that happened during different periods in time barely glimpses the evolution of the cuisine that they ate on a daily basis. However, the fact that descendants of these early people still exist points out that when it came to feeding themselves, the native peoples knew what they were doing long before anyone else came along.

Chapter Two

Native Cuisine Before Cross-Cultural Integration

Now we know that people came to the Northwest and that they ate, and ate well. History about what they ate and how it was prepared is almost nonexistent. In an odd way, this bolsters the previous claim about how well they ate. This statement may seem unneeded, but let me pose the following hypothesis. If you have ever been at a large table where many talented culinarians are voraciously devouring a meal, you would notice the conspicuous lack of verbal banter. This lack of conversation while refueling our bodies has been around as long as man has been able to speak. There is perhaps an argument to be made that we speak the loudest when the sustenance is the least palatable.

This theory has evolved for quite a few millennia. A present-day application would be how loud restaurant reviewers speak when the food is terrible.

On a different level but derived from the same theory, it is easy to conclude when food was good and abundant for early Northwest inhabitants, they would certainly be hesitant about broadcasting this news in fear of attracting anyone or anything that might come to see where this source of the heralded bountiful subsistence originated.

Food was abundant in the Northwest for a few millennia after humans populated the area, and the menu did not change because it did not need to change. There was plenty of food for people to live on. When there was still an abundance of megafauna left to eat during the Paleo-Indian period, these people conducted their lives as nomadic hunter-gatherers in pursuit of large herds of the indigenous animals that inhabited the area. These animals were well suited for the cool, wet climate of the last ice age. The mammoths, mastodons, giant sloths and ancient forms of bison were among the most commonly hunted large game. Projectile points made of bone and obsidian (a glasslike mineral) were found in and near the archaeological remains of these animals, sometimes at sites where significant numbers of them were killed and butchered. Evidence suggests that indigenous vegetation was also an important part of people's diets during the Paleo-Indian period. Solid evidence is rare because delicate plant remains do not preserve very well and are rarely found at Paleo-Indian sites. Therefore, it is difficult for archaeologists to know exactly which plants humans consumed. There is a great likelihood that wild greens, roots, tubers, seeds, nuts and fruits were the staples. The appearance of the previously referenced earth ovens in use some 9,000 years ago might have signaled the dwindling population of megafauna and that changing menus were on the horizon.

Before Western man inserted himself, uninvited, into the habitat of this area, these lands were primarily occupied by many tribes—the Chinook, Salish, Quileute, Quinault and Makah, whose actual name is Qwiqwidicciat.

However, first contact by people from another continent was most likely Asian, not European. According to early Chinese history, a Buddhist monk named Hui Shen described a land he called Fusang, which is most likely North America, placing the discovery of America around AD 500. Yao Silian records many of Hui Shen's findings in the seventh-century text *Book of Liang*.

Recent events solidify the theory of early Asian visitors to North American shores as very plausible and a probable occurrence. The recent event I am referring to is the spring 2012 sighting of what the media has labeled a "Japanese Ghost Ship" (unmanned), drifting toward western British Columbia's shores. It was a fifty-meter fishing vessel that became a casualty of the March 2011 Japanese tsunami. The fact that this ship made it to western North American shores proves that even without power, a ship could drift to North America in a year or so. Another cargo ship left Japan in 1832. It was carrying a cargo of rice, and its rudder was lost at sea, setting it adrift. It, too, arrived on the Pacific Northwest Coast, at Neah Bay in 1834. Therefore, it would not be hard to fathom in AD 500 that the stubborn Buddhist monk Hui Shen successfully made the voyage. By using the same currents, Hui Shen's voyage continued down the coastline to South America, where the currents will take you west again, all the way to China.

In the years after the great migration from Siberia to the Alaskan peninsula, the diet of North America's first inhabitants depended on which route they took south. Among the tribes, there is a dispute surrounding the manner in which they arrived. In particular, the Makah tribe does not consider it a sound belief to assume that all nomadic migrants walked across the Bering Strait land bridge. Current tribal members have emphatically expressed that their arrival was by water. Considering the maritime skills of the Makah peoples, it would be hard to disprove that they arrived on these shores in any manner other than a boat.

The Makahs are a Pacific Northwest Coast tribe notable for being very different from their neighbors. They speak a different language and have many other cultural differences. Whereas other northwestern coastal tribes had either matriarchal or patriarchal linage systems, the Makahs would choose one or the other, depending which lineage would offer the most wealth and family associations. Makahs differ from their Salish neighbors by having an affinity for offshore travel to distances few other coastal tribes were able to traverse. With this seafaring ability, they were able to harvest whales, seals and marine fishes, such as halibut, sea bass, red snapper and rock cod that were more important than the salmon for which the Northwest Coast is renowned. They also consumed sea cucumbers, sea anemones and shrimp—a pretty full menu if you add to it the bounty available on land and in air.

The Northwest's lush and beautiful forests grew tall and dense as the ice age retreated. No place is this more prevalent than where the land ends at Neah Bay, Washington. The red cedar trees that grow here reach sizes not obtained anywhere else, and since few people have ever visited this part of the Northwest, it remains largely the way it was hundreds of years ago. If you arrived at this location by boat a few centuries ago, it would have been a landmark. This is where the continent seems to have split open. Anyone looking for a waterway connection to the East Coast would have headed into this inlet, just as the Greek navigator Juan de Fuca did when he sailed the Spanish expedition in 1592, seeking the fabled Strait of Anian. It would not become the Strait of Juan de Fuca until 1787, when the seafaring captain and maritime fur trader Charles William Barkley renamed it.

Northwest tribal religions hold sacred the giant red cedar because they believe it to be a fundamental gift from the spirits. These trees actually do provide a gift for people restrained in their evolution by the lack of metal tools. The special gift the giant red cedar made available to these peoples was its ability to provide straight-grained wood, which even crude tools could split. The tree that they thought was put here for them would propel these skillful people as they built large houses by tying big slabs of cedar to wooden frames. They made dugout canoes for river travel as well as seagoing whaleboats. From the coasts and rivers of the region, these peoples obtained diverse and abundant food sources. The Northwest provided this subsistence for thousands of years, and the people who settle the coastal areas were fortunate enough to be able to harvest the bounty. In turn, this abundance permitted the development of complex social organizations that placed a premium on ancestry, status and wealth. The components of this society, combined with its spiritual beliefs, founded the artistic traditions through the architecture of each coastal culture. This wealth represents a fundamental difference from other cultures farther inland that figured prominently in the social development of these peoples as they interacted with European explorers.

One significant difference that separates the Makahs from the other northwest coastal peoples was the concept of personal wealth developed through the generous amount of food readily obtainable. This social distinction allowed the Makah people to develop a few traits not commonly found among other early human inhabitants of the Northwest Pacific Coast. Because there was so much available food, some people did not have to gather their own food in order to eat. Those who did could choose to be whalers, fishermen or seal hunters. The gathering of cedar bark was also a task that took on its own role, as they used this material for tools, garments and a multitude of other applications, including the signature look of the time, the cikya·puxs, a hat made of cedar bark that was so tightly knit it was almost waterproof. It has a curiously Asian style that was popular with many of the coastal tribes. Their innovation with materials is also obvious in the ability to fabricate fishing nets from nettles and bone, fishing hooks from wood and harpoon valves from cherry bark.

Just to the south of Neah Bay in La Push, Washington, another coastal tribe—the Quileute—has lived and hunted this area for thousands of years. They are great seafaring people, and they continue to roast fish over fires the way they have for centuries.

Most coastal peoples occupied permanent winter village sites. In the summer, they lived in fixed or portable dwellings while they gathered berries and harvested sea mammals, salmon and other fishes. The social structure of the larger villages included a wealthy elite composed of chiefs or nobles, a body of commoners and slaves, who had no social standing among the tribal hierarchy. The plank houses, as their buildings are called, were integral expressions of these hierarchical cultures. The noble elites, who owned most of the houses, dominated villages. In addition to accommodating extended families, the houses expressed the ancestral heritage and social standing

A view that captures the beauty of First Beach National Park is evident from the Pacific Northwest Quileute Indian Reservation coastline, where rock and driftwood replaces sand at La Push, Washington. *Courtesy of Pamela Heiligenthal.*

of their owners through elaborate totemic imagery in the form of carved posts, painted screens and painted façades. The sheer size of the plank house villages was formidable, with some villages having houses that could reach 150 feet in length extending horizontally on the beach, facing the waves. Several families would live in these houses, and it is where sacred ceremonies, such as the potlatch, would take place. They held potlatches for several reasons: the confirmation of a new chief, coming of age, tattooing or piercing ceremonies, initiation into a secret society, divorce, the funeral of a chief and battle victories. The hosts demonstrated their wealth and prominence through giving away goods. Certain events took place during a potlatch, like singing and dancing, sometimes with masks or regalia. During the ceremony, class structures were reinforced through distribution or sometimes through destruction of property, and material things such as gifts of dried foods, sugar and flour would exchange hands.

The ideology behind a potlatch (and its important lesson we should all take to heart) is the status of any given family is raised not by who has the most resources, but by who distributes the most resources. In our own current social class struggle in the United States, our nation's leader has publically solicited the need for this ideology to become common practice among Americans. Oddly enough, a couple of centuries ago, our government, at the urging of the missionaries, outlawed this ceremony, calling it "a worse than useless custom," that was seen as wasteful, unproductive and contrary to civilized values.

THE BEGINNING OF CROSS-CULTURAL CONTAMINATION

The Spanish established the first European settlement on Makah land in 1792, but this fort lasted only a few months before they abandoned their efforts, leaving behind remnants of their garden for the Makah Nation to find. It was during this period that the Makahs came across the Ozette potato from an abandoned garden, which marked the beginning of cross-cultural contamination.

The Northwest has supported habitation by humans for thousands of years, despite a climate and terrain that, in the sixteenth century, would have appeared to modern Western man as remarkably hostile. Summers are warm but short and devoted to intense outdoor life. The pace is fast with constant hunting and fishing to build up food supplies to last through the coming rains and short days. Winters are long, dark and cold. It was a time characterized by activities that took place primarily indoors. While the history of Salish and other Northwest Native American tribes may go back some 25,000 years or more, knowledge of early cultures and their foodways remains scarce. Other than the mammals, there were quite a few vegetation choices. Plants varied from season to season and from region to region, therefore, people of this period had to travel widely not only in pursuit of game but also to collect their fruits and vegetables. These walkabouts took tribes inevitably into one another's territories, and many of them, after experiencing hostile confrontations, would wisely choose not to take that route again. More often than not, revenge—the downfall of all mankind—would sink its teeth into the souls of the victims. They would become the transgressors, raiding the other tribe's villages and taking slaves to reimburse themselves for the injured and fatally wounded from the earlier skirmish over hunting or fishing grounds. It sounds a bit like an activity that currently takes place in our urban areas. We just call it gang violence—well, except for the slave part. Sometimes as much as we humans change, it seems we don't change at all.

Makah hunters had unique hunting methods for preying on waterfowl. They developed a method in which the birds came to them. They accomplished this challenging method of subsistence by building an elevated cage in their canoes in which they could build a fire. This flame, created while at sea in the rocking waves, would captivate the curiosity of their prey, and the birds would fly close enough for hunters to spear them. I have to say this is one of the most inventive ways of attracting prey while hunting I have ever heard of, and it illuminates the early innovative spirit of the Northwest. Around here, being innovative has been an aspect of Northwest survival for as long as people have been here. If you are not innovative, you are left behind.

Makah people ate a variety of seabirds, including pelicans, loons, cormorants, ducks of various kinds, grebes and divers of various sorts. After being picked and superficially cleaned, the prey was tossed casually into a kettle, then boiled and served up as a feast. As simple as this cooking technique is, combinations of textures and flavors were obviously important, as this next description of a salmonberry stalk combined with salmon roe will demonstrate.

Rubus spectabilis (salmonberry) is an indigenous edible plant that shares the fruit structure of the raspberry. They are tasty eaten raw and when processed into jelly, candy and wine. Native peoples also ate the vitamin-rich young shoots that emerged from the ground as a spring vegetable. Peeled or raw, the shoots taste sweet and juicy and are delicious steamed. The Makahs held salmonberry sprout feasts, singing and dancing on the beach while the sprouts were steam cooked in a pit. One of the most appealing and interesting preparations was a Makah preparation in which they stuffed the sprouts with salmon roe, a luxurious delicacy somewhat similar to celery sticks stuffed with caviar. This dish would have been quite a culinary achievement of taste and texture in a time and place where the impression of luxury was not common or frequent.

Prior to the Spaniards' arrival, the primary source of starch would have been from Wapato roots, sometimes referred to as the duck potato. The leaf stems spring from the base of the plant, celery-like. Below, in the muck, are rhizomes that produce small starchy tubers at their tips. Eaten raw or cooked, the tubers have a similar taste to potatoes or chestnuts prepared in the same fashion. Dried fish would have been the most abundant staple, as it was always on hand as a children's snack or as a base for a stew. The coastal tribe's method of boiling consisted of making waterproof wood boxes of cedar and filling them with water and then heating the water by dropping hot cooking rocks into the boxes. They accomplished seasoning through ingenious methods, such as cooking halibut in salt water and then balancing the seasoning by sweetening with salal berries. These berries were gathered in bulk when they were fresh and then preserved by mashing the fruit and boiling the mash in the cedar boxes. The final step was to press it into cakes and reconstitute them as needed by soaking them in water overnight. When needed, they were broken up and mixed with fish grease for consumption. The salal berries provided a source for sweetening and thickening but were also useful for making dyes and stains. Creative culinary solutions are often born of necessity, and this application brings to light how true that statement actually is.

COASTAL TRIBE EVOLUTION

Among the Northwest coastal peoples, there is evidence of intertribal trading with the Makahs fulfilling the role of facilitators (middlemen), which would make it a natural fit for them to carry out this task with new visitors who came to these shores. This was the first of many changes that would forever alter their lifestyle. Not only were there environmental shifts, but there were also cultural consequences. The trade demand for sea otter and fur seal pelts outstripped the supply in such a short time that the Northwest fur trappers hunted them almost to extinction. Whaling ships from Europe and America depleted the populations of gray and humpback whales so quickly it forced the Makahs to stop hunting whales in the 1920s before the ecosystem completely collapsed.

The cultural consequences caused by the interaction of Western man had an effect on the ancient status system these people had developed from their beginnings. This came about suddenly with the newly found wealth of trade. A man who, in the past, had never accumulated wealth could now change his status in life. Now, with the ability to readily obtain enough wealth to hold potlatches, it was no longer necessary to be the head of a family to redistribute wealth, which caused an upheaval of social structure. With the signing of government treaties, the coastal tribe's evolution would forever change. The populations had dwindled prior to these treaties with the onslaught of diseases the Western man brought, as the native tribe members had no natural antibodies to smallpox, malaria and many other European maladies. These interactions resulted in almost total annihilation of the tribe's existence. In *The Coming of the Spirit of Pestilence* by Robert T. Boyd, it is estimated 88 percent of the coastal populations were decimated by the 1850s. As horrific as the outcome was, neither the coastal tribes nor the visitors from Europe had any knowledge their actions would result in the near extinction of hundreds of thousands of people.

Chapter Three

The Louisiana Purchase

What Did We Get for Our Money?

When discussing this period in history, there seems to be some confusion among the public as to what the objective of the Lewis and Clark expedition actually was. Few know Lewis and Clark did not go to explore the Louisiana Purchase. The expedition was planned before the purchase was made. The Louisiana Purchase was hastened because the port of New Orleans and commerce on the Mississippi River was shut down.

History of Congress records from 1803 allude to the conditions that existed, demonstrating how much it might harm the nation if the Mississippi were closed to commerce. France had only been in possession of the Port of New Orleans for three years when the Spanish closed the port. The convoluted manner in which Napoleon carried out his strategies derived results that even with extended explanations do not make sense to sensible people, with Spain conceding New Orleans back to the French under the condition that it "at no time, under no pretext, and in no manner, be alienated or ceded to any other power." This was an official stipulation in the Third Treaty of San Ildefonso. This stipulation absolutely forbade its sale. Napoleon was not the type of man to respect a treaty, especially if the interest of the moment demanded it to be broken. When that particular moment presented itself to the unscrupulous dictator of France, Napoleon was certainly set to pounce on the opportunity. Not only would he receive some much-needed revenue, but he would also succeed in angering Great Britain in a manner that would tickle his fancy. It would also remove a weak spot in the colonies that France had found troublesome to defend. Napoleon sincerely felt that at some point, the United States would become a maritime rival that could defeat the British, and this thought pleasured him immensely. President Jefferson felt that the purchase was of the utmost importance, and expedience in concluding the transaction was extremely urgent. Once France took back possession of the territories from Spain, the threat of war in New Orleans was suddenly a good possibility. France now posed a potential threat to America. With France gaining control of the Port of New Orleans and Napoleon filled with the pride of his latest conquests in Europe, he suddenly desired an expansion of France in the New World. There was a fear that if America did not purchase New Orleans from France, it could lead to war. Several attempts were made by France and Britain to encourage separatist movements among the American settlers of the western states, and Jefferson feared the unity of the nation was at stake. The change of ownership at this key port resulted in its closing. American commerce traveling down the Mississippi River and into the Gulf of Mexico came to a grinding halt.

Realizing the expedience of the situation, Jefferson nominated James Monroe on January 11, 1803, to be the envoy to go and help U.S. minister to France Robert Livingston seal the deal and negotiate the transaction with Napoleon's negotiator, French foreign minister Charles Talleyrand. These events dictated the pace, and now things needed to happen quickly. Monroe was to secure the purchase of whatever he could (the city, the territory or the port) so as not to hinder commerce on the Mississippi. Instead, they returned with an agreement to buy the entire Louisiana Territory for the sum of $12 million (60 million francs). In addition, the United States canceled some French debt (close to $4 million), bringing the total price to $15 million U.S.

America did not have the money to pay the $12 million, so we borrowed the money from Great Britain. Why they would ever loan it to us is beyond me. Looking back, it seems odd that the United States would borrow money from England, considering the United States had been at war with the British only a couple of decades prior and would return to war with England in 1812. The actual Louisiana Purchase included what would become thirteen states. They are Missouri, Arkansas, Oklahoma, Louisiana, Kansas, Colorado, Nebraska, Iowa, Minnesota, Wyoming, Montana, South Dakota and North Dakota. Curiously missing are Utah, Idaho, Oregon and Washington.

NAPOLEON

Insane Dictator or Culinary Snob?

The Third Treaty of San Ildefonso (named for the king's summer palace) was a secretly negotiated treaty between France and Spain in which Spain returned the colonial territory of Louisiana to France. Since the terms of the treaty did not specify territory boundaries being returned, this caused a point of contention between Spain and the United States.

Remarkably, French culinary traditions played a large part in this monumental transaction. French impressions of what could be grown here to eat had a major part in influencing Napoleon to make the actual real estate transfer. Prior to the transfer of ownership from Spain to France, Napoleon sent François André Michaux to America to study the value of the plant life and trees of this land. Michaux also had a covert mission to inspire American pioneers to take up arms against Spain. Michaux reported to Napoleon that France should clear the bulk of the American lands since most of the natural vegetation was worthless. Michaux felt that France grew superior plants, and it is thought that Napoleon's decision to sell the land to President Jefferson at a mere four cents per acre was somewhat determined by Michaux's reports. Well, that and Napoleon really hated the British and would do anything to anger them anytime he could. He also knew the Americans would soon overrun the lands west of the Mississippi, so he might as well get paid what he could for it. With the purchase of this new territory, the land area of what would become the United States nearly doubled in size. However, the exact southern and western boundaries were undefined in the purchase. America would have to work with Spain on the boundary details. Nevertheless, with the usual irony of ignorance, we would not let a couple of loose ends or undefined details keep us from forging ahead. Some of the most miraculous events in our country's history happen from this dedication to the delirium of greatness.

One of the amazing things about the Lewis and Clark journey is the insistence that the Columbia River would lead to a connection to the fabled Northwest Passage. This conjecture—with our limited knowledge of the land between St. Louis, Missouri, on the Mississippi River and Astoria, Oregon, on the mouth of the Columbia River—was quite a leap of faith, especially considering the limited maps of the Rocky Mountains. The knowledge Captain James Cook obtained by the time he made his third voyage in 1780 helped Jefferson put together in his mind a mental map of the continent. They also had Captain Gray's 1790s account of sighting what he thought was the Northwest Passage connection, even though the British captain George Vancouver did not share the same opinion, as shown here in his daily journal from April 28, 1792, after a chance meeting with Gray:

> *The several large rivers and capacious inlets that have been described as discharging their contents into the Pacific between the 40th and 48th degree north latitude, were reduced to brooks insufficient for our vessels to navigate, or to bays inapplicable for refitting.*

Known for his overland crossing of what is now Canada to reach the Pacific Ocean in 1793, Alexander Mackenzie, a Scottish explorer, conducted a journey that predated the Lewis and Clark expedition by ten years. Many relied on his experiences as a reference to what was out there in this uncharted wilderness. President Jefferson combined the three explorers' findings to conclude that the continent was about three thousand miles wide—a good guesstimate working from the information he had to go on. This would provide the base for tallying the amount of provisions necessary to the success of the expedition, an assessment that would provide a recipe for success.

It Is Going to Be a Long Bumpy Ride

When examined with a mature bit of scrutiny, our history on this continent takes on a meaning not quite aligned with the historical facts I was educated and armed with before I went out into society. Much of the information we have held as the basis of what we know about how the Northwest developed is, to say the least, skewed and, at the worst, a travesty of historical importance. The Louisiana Purchase did not include Oregon Country as it was referred to, and the Oregon Territory (what it came to be known as) included what is now Washington State. It later became two separate territories and then two separate states. Oregon became a state in 1859, and Washington was admitted into the union in 1889. The order in which Jefferson described the purchase to Congress when nominating Monroe put a bit of a spotlight on Jefferson's real intentions. Before Monroe set sail to negotiate the deal, Jefferson moved to acquire all of Louisiana, including the vast expanse that included what is now Oregon. This clearly places the Pacific Northwest territory as the primary goal of the Louisiana Purchase.

As we examine this journey, it is hard to fathom that only 208 years ago our culture was so different from what it is today. How often we decry the actions of others when only two centuries ago we were guilty of committing many of the same atrocities we hold in such contempt. One such atrocity was the consumption of canines. This fact, as shocking as it may seem, is verifiable information. As unpleasant as it is to read, it did actually happen. It is hard to imagine only 200 years ago, some of our country's larger-than-life historical and cultural heroes, men who were from educated and privileged backgrounds, ate dogs. Not hot dogs, but dogs bought from Native Americans. The official list of game consumed on the expedition lists 190 dogs purchased and consumed. In fact, Captain Lewis professed to prefer the flesh of dog meat to that of venison or elk. However, Captain William Clark abstained from consuming canine flesh. I have never personally eaten dog meat, so it is hard for me to offer an opinion here. But I have to say it must taste pretty good because I have worked at restaurants that served venison and elk, and I cannot imagine preferring dog to elk or venison.

History and geography were two of my favorite subjects in school, and I paid close attention and had what I thought were good teachers. It was astonishing to find out educators left out many of the details I read from the Lewis and Clark journals. I started to survey my friends from San Francisco to Boston to see what they remembered from their education about the Lewis and Clark expedition and found I was not alone. It seems as though southern public schools were not the only ones who left out many of the facts.

It is not exactly a well-known fact that Meriwether Lewis was secretary to the President for two years before leaving on the Lewis and Clark expedition. Soon-to-be President Jefferson knew Captain Lewis and his family because they were both from Virginia. Captain Lewis attended the same school that Jefferson did and was close enough to Meriwether Lewis to know exactly where he was in February 1801, a month before Jefferson's inauguration. Newly elected President Jefferson transferred Captain Lewis from the First Infantry to become the secretary to the president.

This expedition was obviously on Thomas Jefferson's mind for quite some time before it came to fruition. Within a couple of days of becoming president of the United States, Jefferson summoned Lewis to his quarters, where he became intimately aware of all that embodied the proposal that would become President Jefferson's secret message to Congress on January 18, 1803.

A Secret Message to Congress

Thomas Jefferson's secret request for appropriation went against what he had already told Spain's foreign minister Marques de Casa Yrujo. As president of the United States, Thomas Jefferson played a major role regarding agriculture and viticulture trends, and centuries later, those cultural commitments still reverberate through current times, influencing what we drink and eat today. A good example is the 2011 Wine Bloggers Conference. The main dining event for this prestigious affair took place on the grounds of Jefferson's mansion Monticello in Virginia.

To discuss this monumental excursion with any authority, it might be good to begin by defining what the Louisiana Territory actually was and why we negotiated with Spain to explore the region but bought the land from France. The first explanation might be difficult because defining the physical location of what the Louisiana Territory consisted of in actual boundaries depends on whom you were asking. Jefferson's understanding of what defined Louisiana was the forty-ninth parallel to the north and farther north if the Missouri River drainage basin extended higher than forty-nine degrees. The eastern boundary was the Mississippi River, the southern was the Gulf of Mexico and the western was the Continental Divide. At this time, this particular boundary was still a hypothetical conception. Some believed that south of the forty-ninth parallel and north of undefined California, Louisiana extended past the Continental Divide and all the way to the Pacific Ocean.

When President Jefferson asked Spain's foreign minister Marques De Casa Yrujo in November 1802 if the Spanish court would take it badly if he sent a small expedition party to explore the course of the Missouri River, he already had a plan. When Jefferson proposed the expedition, he specifically stated it would be for the advancement of commerce. But in reality, the objective was to advance the geography of the United States. This coast-to-coast expansion would secure our future against invasion by England, Spain and France and many other agendas that were only a twinkling of an idea in the mind of our president at that time—a big leap considering President Jefferson did not know how and when he could secure the West Coast.

In his original conversation with Minister Yrujo, he did however mention the intent to observe the territories between forty and sixty degrees parallel from the mouth of the Missouri River to the Pacific Ocean. The master plan reflected an idea that had been around for three centuries but never accomplished—searching for the Northwest Passage that would make a transoceanic route from the Pacific to the Atlantic possible. Although the Louisiana Purchase did not include the Oregon Territory, the territory that included what is now Washington State, the Treaty of 1818 would finalize our northern border at forty-nine degrees. It later became two separate territories and then two separate states.

MAKING SURE THEY KNEW WHERE THEY WERE GOING

Lewis needed quite a bit of education on the use of navigational equipment and received a serviceable amount of information regarding the correct and accurate operation of these instruments, primarily the sextant, chronometer and compass. While receiving his training and procuring equipment, Lewis realized he would need another officer and more men than the dozen called for in the original expedition plan. Lewis knew early on that he wanted his friend Captain Clark who he had served with in the past. Clark had since relinquished his military commissioning, and getting him the rank of captain back proved easier said than done. Lewis knew that in order for the men to respect their leadership equally, Clark would need equal rank. Returning to the frontier at the age of thirty-three, Lewis knew Captain Clark was the man for the job, and those who doubted him would soon have nothing but admiration for him once he triumphantly returned from the expedition. A better-matched pair for the job at hand would have been impossible to find. Captain Clark had superior Native American knowledge and was a natural with the men without becoming friendly. He was also a better river man that Captain Lewis. Most importantly, Lewis trusted him explicitly.

Completing the required provisions for the trip proved more time consuming than Captain Lewis anticipated. Most difficult was getting delivery of a keelboat that Clark contracted to have built by a drunken boat builder in Fredericktown, Maryland. The contract specified that the boat be finished by July 20, 1803, before the depth of the Ohio River was too low to navigate. In the meantime, Captain Clark started his search for the men who would become "the Corps of Discovery." This endeavor became an arduous task as finding frontiersmen who could work the river and survive the wilderness proved to be challenging. Finally, the boat was finished, and as a testament to how anxious Lewis was to get going, on August 31, after the last nail went into the boat at 7:00 a.m., by 10:00 a.m. the boat was fully loaded. They were on their way—well, sort of.

And They Were Off

Lewis only traveled three miles down the Ohio toward the Mississippi when pioneers of the area summoned the boat to come ashore so they could view the unusual firearm the expedition acquired from the Philadelphia gunsmith Isaiah Lukens. The weapon, a pump air rifle, was unique for that time period. The stock could hold enough air pressure to have a charge not much inferior to that of a Kentucky rifle, and it made no noise or smoke. The travels of this expedition were popular discussion, and settlers living in an age of only mail and newspapers seemed to be abreast of the movements and aware of when the expedition would travel past. At this first stop, Lewis learned a valuable lesson about firearm safety. Lewis demonstrated the rifle by firing it accurately at a range of fifty-five yards, impressing all who had come to see it. While passing the air rifle around for people to view after the demonstration, it accidentally discharged, striking a woman in the temple and lacerating the skin to a degree that Lewis thought it had killed her. It would be the last time he allowed anyone to handle the rifle pressurized and loaded to fire.

Around a hundred miles down the Ohio River, Lewis arrived in Clarksville, Indiana territory. On the opposite bank is Louisville, Kentucky. It is here where Lewis and Clark were reunited, and the expedition officially started. At this time, Clark was a little worried about the Sioux because he heard from Americans living at the mouth of the Missouri River that they were a large, well-armed and formidable force of hostile men who would certainly demand payment for passage through their territory. This concern prompted the captains to purchase one brass cannon and mount it on a swivel aboard the keelboat. If a conflict with the Sioux (or any other Plains tribe for that matter) occurred and things did not go well, they would be giving up the largest cache of arms to have ever crossed the Mississippi River. If those arms changed hands, the balance of power would have changed, creating a scenario in which the westward expansion of our country would have been almost impossible.

At the beginning of the expedition, Lewis made comments about how much he enjoyed the taste of a well-fried fat squirrel. Lewis reminisced fondly of the times when he hunted squirrels on the banks of the Ohio River with his dog, named Seaman. Lewis's dog was a large black Newfoundland he paid twenty dollars for, which was quite a steep price for a dog back then, and considering the propensity frontiersmen had for consuming canines, it was an unusual decision to bring the dog on the excursion. I find the respect and reverence he displayed at this time for his dog Seaman quite ironic and the mention of eating squirrels not so remarkable. In fact, I will have to agree with Captain Lewis here because on more than one occasion I have enjoyed the flesh of a well-fried squirrel. While educating himself for this mission, Lewis had quite the social life dining at statesmen's parties, where he would consume the finest food and wine afforded to anyone in the country at that time, a pleasure he would later lament in his journals while freezing in the rain on the Northwest Coast.

A reoccurring theme regarding what people ate and how the progression of new species and innovative cooking techniques came into play affirms the Lewis Binford theory, which states, "In times of privation, people will move to smaller game, then to aquatic resources, and then to root foods as a natural progression of survival." This seemed to be the operational theory for the Lewis and Clark expedition and it seemed to happen, as Binford mentions, as a natural progression instead of a thought-out plan of action.

Speaking of what people ate, although President Jefferson did not fuss over the way he dressed, he did keep the finest table, an attribute that has carried on in the White House now for more than two centuries. Many of the recipe books written about the Lewis and Clark expedition spend a great deal focusing on the meals that Lewis would consume while in the company of the president. While these stories are interesting, they are not pertinent to this story. The foods that kept the men alive after they left the winter camp of Fort Mandan in the early spring of 1805 and the bounty of yet undiscovered foods as they reached the Pacific Ocean will illuminate this expedition of northwestern cuisine. The interaction with all the diverse cultures of the many inhabitants occupying the lands they crossed would help define the evolution of culinary compromise these men would endure. The tougher the times got and the scarcity of familiar things to eat would change how they viewed sustenance while bolstering the ability to embrace the unknown. In anyone's life, if you reach this point of letting go of what you know, you will gain new knowledge that will help you grow. In their case, it was as physical as it was spiritual.

PORTABLE SOUP, WHO KNEW?

Numerous sources report that Lewis received $2,500 from Congress to obtain supplies, materials and services needed for the expedition. Additionally,

Jefferson gave Lewis a letter of credit to obtain goods and services, in which Lewis spent almost $39,000—equivalent to $750,000 in today's money. Jefferson opened up the full resources of the United States for materials, and Lewis took full advantage. When I first saw the figure, I thought it meant the cost of subsistence provisions for the trip, and after seeing the list of food and alcohol purchased and how much game they hunted while on the expedition, I thought it had to be wrong. There were only forty-five people involved and there is no way they spent the equivalent of three-quarters of a million dollars to feed forty-five people for a couple of years. The figure quoted was not just for sustenance but included all other provisions.

Weapons, medical supplies, clothing, camp equipment, medicine, gifts for the Native Americans and food would have been included in those purchases. Curiously, among the list of provisions, two items perked my interest. The first is a nod to Lewis for having spent two years prior living at the president's house (now called the White House). It seems Lewis eschewed purchasing the amount of whiskey provisioned and instead chose strong spirit wine (brandy), something that would have been common in the liquor cabinet of the former ambassador to France. The other oddity was the 193 pounds of "portable soupe," which Lewis described on September 18, 1805, while the corps was in the Bitterroot Mountains:

> We dined & supped on a skant [sic] proportion of portable soupe, a few canesters [sic] of which, a little bears oil and about 20 lbs. of candles form our stock of provision.

This was quite a revelation to this culinarian, who had no idea that bouillon (these days called soup base) was around way back then. In the late seventeenth century, a Frenchman invented it, and it became a standard for the British navy. This invention was a lifesaver on the expedition, keeping the men from starving on a couple of occasions.

Ohio, Mississippi, Missouri

Many Rivers to Cross

With many miles crossed and many more to go, the expedition was far from starting. They did, however, catch a 128-pound catfish on November 16,

1803. It would have yielded over a pound of edible catfish per man. It is not unusual to catch even larger catfish as heavy as 200 pounds where the Mississippi and Ohio Rivers converge. It does not become an exploration until you are exploring uncharted territory—well, at least when you do it for the government.

The time spent at the convergence of the Ohio and Mississippi Rivers was a necessary diversion for the corps. Finalization of all supplies and personnel would take place soon. Meanwhile, Lewis honed his skills with the celestial instruments, practicing his ability to plot longitude and latitude and taking accurate measurements so he could produce maps. Seeking and obtaining an audience with James Mackay was imperative. Mackay was a Scottish trader and explorer who made it all the way up the Missouri to the village of the Omahas in 1795, and the following year, he sent a young assistant named John Evans to find the Pacific Ocean. He only made it as far as the Mandan Villages. In 1803, Mackay was living in St. Louis, so Lewis had the opportunity to meet with him and speak about his map. Now Lewis was in possession of the most information any white man before him had obtained of the Missouri country and a little information about what the Native Americans knew of the lands that lie to the west.

The fur trade was already prospering in St. Louis, and it did not matter if it was Spain or France who claimed to own the property. It became apparent to Captain Lewis if America was going to profit from the bounty of the western lands, his mission's success would be critical.

Chapter Four

Lewis and Clark

The Expedition of Northwest Cuisine

THE EXPEDITION BEGINS

On May 22, 1804, Lewis and Clark launched the keelboat, and the men headed up the Missouri, arriving at Daniel Boone's settlement on the Missouri River a few days later. Daniel Boone had received from the Spanish government a land grant obtaining acreage in Missouri because by the start of the nineteenth century, Kentucky had become too crowded for a frontiersman of Mr. Boone's nature. At Boone's Missouri settlement, the expedition went into town to meet Daniel Boone, and they also bought fresh butter and corn. The villagers gifted the expedition some fresh milk and eggs. It is safe to say that whatever the entree was for the next couple of evenings (most likely venison or catfish), some sort of baked goods, sweet pastries and any other dishes that would make good use of milk and eggs more than likely accompanied the meal.

The party continued upriver, meeting several trappers who shared knowledge of the river and the movement of the Sioux. The prevalent source of protein was deer. This food source seemed to be the type of sustenance the hunters returned with daily and the crew tired of easily. There is not much discussion in the journals of Lewis and Clark about making use of wild herbs to bolster the flavor of boiled venison. Without salt, pepper or spices of any kind, boiled game is not very palatable after the fourth or fifth meal. Although the portable soup would have been a great addition to use in braised venison, it was necessary to save it for times when there was absolutely nothing else to eat.

Lewis and Clark Journals. *Courtesy of Pamela Heiligenthal.*

On May 26, 1804, Lewis issued detachment orders to establish the routines of the men. These documents also establish that this was a military expedition, which would lead into hostile territory. Any Native American contact could become a confrontation that might impede President Jefferson's objectives. Those objectives were primarily to explore newly acquired territory, find a water route to the Pacific Ocean and, most importantly, establish an American claim to the Oregon Country. The detachment orders also outlined guard duty and stressed the importance of alertness. They divided the party into three squads or messes. Each evening upon landing, the Sergeant of Arms would issue each mess the day's provisions. They would cook it at once, and a portion was reserved for the following day. There was no food preparation allowed during the day. The ration was usually hominy and lard on one day and salt pork and flour for the next. Whatever game the hunters brought in, they would divvy up, and on those days, no lard or pork would be issued. In the first five days of June, the hunters brought in about twenty deer. After eating what they could of the fresh meat, what they could not consume would be "jerked," as they called it, which meant to dry and prepare as jerky. Other than a bit of watercress here and there and the occasional spotting of wild greens, the men were not getting very much in the way of vegetation in their diets at this point. Fresh signs of an Indian party of roughly ten men were spotted but no actual Indians yet. You can bet each time they came close, the party was on heightened alert, and they would check for weapon readiness.

On June 11, 1804, the expedition's hunters brought in the first bear. Although the journals mention they killed two bears and one deer and made jerky with most of the meat, there is no reference to how the first bear was cooked. Most likely, it was either spit-roasted or boiled. The corps was making about twenty miles a day at this point heading upstream in boats without any method to propel them other than oars, pushrods or manually attaching a cable to the keelboat's mast. Each sign of downstream movement was cause for alarm. Constant awareness of what or who was coming toward the party was necessary. Now several hundred miles upriver, the party had not encountered any Indians, but when they did, they did not want to startle them or appear to be threatening.

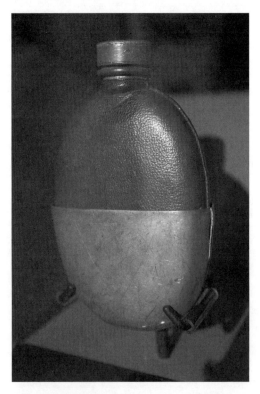

A metal flask used by a member on the Lewis and Clark expedition. *Courtesy of Pamela Heiligenthal.*

On June 26, 1804, now four hundred miles upriver, where the Missouri meets the Kansas River, the party had completed the western trek across what would become the state of Missouri. Here, they would camp for four days, making observations. A few days later, the party prepared to ready themselves to enter back into the river and proceed upstream. They did not adhere to this schedule because of the events that took place that evening. Disciplinary issues arose among the men because there had been a raid on the supply of spirits. Private Collins, who was on guard duty, tapped a barrel of the brandy, and after a few drinks, Private Hall came upon him. Collins offered Hall a drink, and he accepted. Later, they were both drunk. Shortly after that, the sergeant at arms placed them both under arrest. This breach of security was relevant enough to delay the embarkation. It caused a need to take stock of the alcohol inventory, and they soon discovered there were only 104 days of brandy left in reserve, according to Lewis's calculations of the daily ration of a gill per man per day. This would mean the whiskey would be gone around early October 1804. It is doubtful that they would encounter any source to obtain spirits, making it a bit of a conundrum as to how they still had alcohol on July 4, 1805. This excerpt from *Ardent Spirits on the Expedition* by Robert R. Hunt offers a plausible explanation:

> *On May 18, 1804, Clark records in his journal that two keelboats arrive from Kentucky loaded with whiskey, hats, etc. Can the reader assume that the boat carried cargo for delivery to the expedition, or is Clark merely observing commercial civilian traffic on the river? This reference may have been a basis for an assumption that these boats delivered their "whiskey, hats, etc." to Lewis and Clark. At least one commentator, Rochonne Abrams, alleges that the expedition carried 300 gallons of spirits. That clearly disputes the accepted figure of 120 gallons and puts forth a theory that coincides with the amounts consumed and how long the alcohol would last.*

The men were well aware now that there would not be enough alcohol to make it to the Pacific and back, even if they watered down what they had left. They drew official charges against Privates Hall and Collins and a court convened. Found guilty, they sentenced the privates to fifty lashes each. Flogging was a common occurrence among slave owners and military men. The punishment fit the crime, as it required the other party members to carry out the lashings. It allowed the men to express their anger in an immediate and physical manner for the indiscretions of the perpetrators, especially when pilferage of the alcohol was the crime. If you drank my share of alcohol, I would certainly want to hand out the punishment. The men knew the alcohol would not last the entire journey, and they were OK with that, as long as they all ran out together and everyone got an equal share. Eager to get on its way, the party departed although Privates Collins and Hall were sore rowing up the river with the wounds inflicted from the floggings. The two transgressors were not the only physically afflicted crew, as it is noted that many of the crew had developed skin eruptions such as boils and tumors, which they thought were the consequence of drinking the river water. Hey, nobody said this would be pretty. The consumption of vegetables had diminished to almost nothing, resulting in the onset of scurvy, and the constant blanketing of mosquitoes and other insects played a large role in the declining physical condition of the Corps. But they rowed on upstream defiant and determined.

Unexploited Plains Bring Garden of Eden Bounty

As they crossed the twenty-third meridian, the feeling of being in the land of Eden was strong due to the wondrous beauty of unexploited plains and the uninhabited spaces these explorers were discovering by the moment. The unparalleled bounty of game, which consisted mostly of deer, elk, buffalo and the occasional pesky bear, most certainly would have left an impression on the corps that few men would have experienced then or since. The fruit grew wild and abundantly, but green, root or starchy vegetables were rare.

On July 4, 1804, the crew celebrated Independence Day with a couple of firings from the cannon, one at dawn and another at dusk, and an extra gill of spirits. Four days later, disciplinary actions were required once again but not for stealing whiskey. This time, the infraction was much more serious. It was for sleeping on guard while in Sioux territory. These days, if you fell asleep while on military guard duty in hostile territory, it is an offense that carries the death penalty. That punishment is usually reserved for soldiers who fell asleep and allowed enemy combatants to take the lives of their fellow countrymen without the benefit of being forewarned by the soldier who had been posted on guard duty.

Having traveled 680 miles upriver on the Missouri River, no Indians had been seen so far. All the tribes were away hunting buffalo on the prairie at that time. At this point, the expedition has entered Sioux territory, and they are on heightened alert. Captain Clark's birthday arrived on August 1without much fanfare from the men. This is when being in charge is good. Clark ordered up a menu that was achievable and delicious: a saddle of venison, a fleece of elk and the tail of a beaver, culminating with a fresh fruit desert of cherries, raspberries, plums, currants and grapes. For the next few days, they enjoyed the fresh fruit and prepared to meet with the local tribes. Captain Lewis had been waiting for this day to come for quite some time. This was the day he would give his first speech to the Native Americans, a speech he had practiced many times and had been coached on by the White House staff. None of his preparations were adequate to convey properly

42

what he needed to say. It was only by luck that they were fortunate enough to not have been killed. The translations were fragmented and inaccurate.

The journal entries on August 15, 1804, speak of the amount of fish the men were able to harvest by just dragging a net made of willow and bark through the water of a creek where beavers had made a dam. They caught over three hundred fish—pike, perch, catfish and, oddly enough, crawfish and mussels. It is the second mention of the abundance of fish available on the river whenever they wanted them. This deviation from an almost all red meat diet would have been a welcomed one among the men. Monotony in the diet of military men can lead to unrest, and that is never a good thing. A creative cook can always be useful and, on occasion, a real savior. This statement is just as true today as it was back then. Of note, Lewis and Clark were the first to describe the following fish: white sturgeon, goldeye, blue catfish, channel catfish, Columbia River chub, mountain sucker, starry flounder, northern squawfish, cutthroat trout, steelhead trout, sauger and eulachon (also known as candlefish).

On August 23, 1804, Private Joseph Field killed the Corp of Discovery's first buffalo in what is now South Dakota. This would have been a memorable dining experience and a first for most of the men on the expedition. The hump and tongue were the cuts preferred by the men. The only other delicacy they enjoyed consuming as much was the tail of the beaver cooked over an open fire. They jerked the leftover meat, which meant deboning and drying, and they would use the hides for garments or construction. On a personal level, no one laments this day ever came to pass as much as I do. This moment marked the initiation of the annihilation of our buffalo herds on the plains by the white man. I am certain if the Plains tribes knew the magnitude of things to come, they would have killed every member of the Corps of Discovery right then and there, starting with Captain Lewis and Captain Clark.

Once again, the concept that only bad things happen when you have a bounty of riches and others find out about it comes into play here. The plains tribes could be aggressive and violent toward anyone encroaching on their hunting and gathering activities. The infiltration of English and French fur traders from the north and the earlier explorations of the Spaniards put these tribes on notice, and it did not help that these European antagonists would attempt to manipulate whomever they could to battle any tribe that did not want to do business with them. Instigating wars between the tribes was just a way of doing business for the fur traders, who looked on the Native Americans as savages.

There was always danger lurking for the members of the expedition, and sometimes, it was not exactly obvious as to how deadly the danger actually was. As scientific as Captain Lewis was, he had a habit of tasting unknown substances to identify them. In this case, what was thought to be cobalt was actually arsenic. We, as humans, developed taste receptors to help us identify substances that may kill us. Lewis obviously took this fact of evolution very literally.

On September 23, the corps's northwest movement was noticed by some young Lakota Sioux boys, who immediately set off the warning alarm (they set the prairie on fire). Both captains noticed the smoke behind them and knew the Sioux were well aware of their presence. When they stopped to set up camp for the night, the boys arrived and informed them they had warned their tribe that the expedition was approaching. The boys divulged where their villages were and how many people lived there—most likely to boast of their strength. The captains gave the boys some tobacco to take to the chief with a request for a meeting. The civilized manner in which these meetings or councils were arranged is somewhat surprising. However, when you consider that the expedition knew the villages were on the river and they needed to pass them, announcing their arrival was prudent.

The expedition had its first official council with the Sioux on September 25, 1804, at the mouth of the Teton River. It was not received well. Known as pirates of the river, the Sioux would charge exorbitant fees to pass upriver. Lewis and Clark had known this day would come when the Sioux would proposition them as they levied their charge for continuing up the Missouri River. This exchange usually consisted of the Sioux naming a price they would pay for the goods, which amounted to nothing. They carried out this charade because the Sioux did not want to be called thieves but instead shrewd negotiators. The two parties met at 11:00 a.m. First, gifts exchanged were buffalo meat the Sioux brought. In turn, the captains brought some pork as gifts. They proceeded to smoke, as was the custom, and then Lewis gave his speech. Had Twitter been in existence this particular Tuesday, we could give it the hashtag #TTT (Trash Talking Tuesday). The trash talking could have spun out of control, but without adequate translators, they could only accomplish so much verbal banter for better or for worse.

Lewis invited the chiefs onto the keelboat because he thought it advantageous to let them look at such curiosities they had never seen before. After the captains made the mistake of offering whiskey, things got a little dicey. Alcohol given to anyone who has not experienced it tends to generate negative experiences, which may be amplified if alcohol has not been in your social structure for many generations.

After receiving gifts from the captains, the Sioux expressed the gifts were not enough and attempted to extort a fee for allowing the party to proceed up river. At this point, they told the expedition it could return down river with what it had, or it could leave behind one of its boats with all of its goods to continue up the river. One of the chiefs stated just as the expedition had men and weapons so did they and that they had more men in the villages upriver that would stand against the expedition. Captain Clark in return expressed to them that on the boat, he had men and medicine that could kill twenty such nations in a day. Captain Lewis was now angry and determined to convince the Teton Sioux that white men would defend themselves and commit violent acts if necessary. Captain Clark stood with his saber drawn ready for a fight, and Captain Lewis stood ready to ignite the fuse on the cannon. Several of the Teton Sioux warriors grabbed the rope of the keelboat refusing to let go until they received more tobacco. The chief was surprised at their defensive behavior over what little they had asked for and again insults were hurled. This tense moment ended with Lewis offering his hand in friendship to the chief, who refused it. In return, Lewis got back in the boat to head back to the keelboat. As he pushed off, a couple of the chiefs waded into the water and asked if they could come aboard. Captain Lewis obliged, most likely in an attempt to keep his enemies close, which most likely was the same reason the chiefs wanted to sleep on the boat that night, too.

The expedition traveled upriver a short way to spend the night under heavy guard. Lewis did not sleep well and named the island where they docked and camped for the night "Bad Humor Island" to reflect his present mood. As they proceeded up the river the following morning, members of this tribe lined the banks for four miles. The Sioux arranged to take a different approach by showing some hospitality in order to attempt negotiations again. On September 26, the Teton Sioux performed an activity of pageantry called the scalp dance—a dance where enemies' scalps obtained in attacks are paraded by the tribe's wives, probably in hopes of impressing the expedition with their ability to conquer their enemies. This event was a prestigious celebration, and the menu held many surprises and delicacies. First, a fine soup made of white apples—aka, the prairie turnip (*Psoralea esculenta*)—was offered and appreciated. Captain Clark referred to it as "only a bit inferior," a style of praise in the jargon of the time, which meant it was pretty good. The courses that followed consisted of buffalo served three ways—fatty braised buffalo brisket, dried and pounded pemmican, and buffalo bone marrow, considered quite a delicacy at the time. The next course—spit roasted canine—was considered by the Sioux as the ultimate delicacy. The crew obviously loved this dish, as it would become one of their favorites over the next couple of years.

Lack of communication and trash talking went hand in hand, however, it is hard to accomplish the latter if you do not have a translator who can communicate sufficiently. Both sides exchanged gifts. However, the Sioux thought they should receive more. In their minds, the Sioux thought it only fitting to demand payment to proceed farther on the river. It was just their way of doing business. A confrontation ensued but nobody died and nobody went to jail, the standard I use to decide whether or not it was a good day.

Just as quickly as the Sioux were warned that the white men were approaching, the outcome of the confrontations between the Corps of Discovery and the Teton Sioux raced across the plains far in advance of the corps itself. The ability to face down the mighty Sioux without violence sent a message that these white men were different from any white men the Plains tribes had ever dealt with before. Continuing without confrontation was all they were looking for and it seems that message was well received.

With a good east or south wind blowing, the expedition was able to proceed upriver under sail in the keelboat. Weather was changing as fall approached, and they were still heading north on the river. To say the mornings were brisk is probably an understatement. It would have been very cold heading northwest on the Missouri River at that time of the year. This drop in temperature was only a small taste of things to come as these men headed into what would become the coldest winter any of them would ever experience. As the expedition proceeded upriver, members of different tribes came out to meet them without incident. Most of the interactions were requests for food or tobacco, which they obliged, and gun powder, which they refused for obvious reasons.

On October 10, 1804, the council with the Arikaras took place. These people had never seen a black man before and were quite amused by Captains Clark's servant, York. Much to the dismay of the captains, York entertained the tribe, telling them that before Captain Clark found him he was wild and ate people. He then referred to how good children were to eat. The tribe bestowed on the expedition gifts of corn, watermelon, squash, pumpkins and beans. The particular bean that was given as a gift was pretty special in its own right. The Plains tribes would steal this bean (*Amphicarpaea monoica*), also known as the American hog peanut, from the white-footed mouse and other rodents. The Plains tribes would leave other food for the mice when they took this bean, often used for its seeds to cultivate the beans. Sustainability was a concept these people had practiced for their entire existence.

Many other tribes relied on the Arikaras for their supply of corn, as did some of the European fur traders. The captains discovered (without incident) that this tribe was not fond of liquor of any kind. Had they been offered a fine Bordeaux or Burgundy, who knows, it might have been a different story. That offer of wine could have been a possibility, as they discovered large amounts of wild grapes growing in this location. With the liquor supply dwindling and plenty of ripe fruit to source, it is a mystery that they did not start some fermentation of juice, especially considering Lewis's scientific background.

Captain Lewis made his usual speech to all tribes they met, seeking to make peace and to promote trade. The message was well received, and they in return expressed a desire to be at peace with all nations. In response, the chief declared the road was open and that no one from his nation would dare attempt to delay the expedition's progress. This was a clear indication that communication moved upriver very fast and that the confrontation with the Sioux had preceded their arrival. The Arikaras requested the expedition take one of their chiefs on board to travel with the corps to the next village, where the Mandan tribe lived. At the time, they were at war with the Mandans and wanted to restore peace. They hoped that Captain Lewis would be able to broker that peace between the tribes.

Keeping the peace among the men at this point had become a point of contention to the captains, who were forced to administer disciplinary action against Private Newman because he had made mutinous and criminal statements. Any soldier, who affects the general morale, especially during what many would have considered combat operations, cannot be tolerated and must go. A court-martial (jury) was formed, and a sentence of discipline was issued. Sentenced to seventy-five lashes, the jury banished Newman from the party. On October 13, 1804, with rain falling, they assembled the men and the lashes were given. Upon viewing the punishment, the Arikara Chief traveling on the boat wept openly. When the captains inquired, he responded that even though he had sent men to death in battle and understood the necessity of discipline, it was their custom not to strike each other. They did not even strike their children. This revelation probably influenced the mission to a degree no one would ever completely comprehend. Just as the news that the corps faced down the mighty Sioux traveled across the plains like wildfire, news of white men who would commit violent acts against their own men if they stepped out of line probably caused quite a stir. This fact set the stage for the travels of the expedition throughout the rest of the trip.

In October, the expedition saw its first grizzly bear. All previously sighted or killed bears were black bears. In their journals, Lewis and Clark refer to the grizzly as a white bear. They also saw the destruction epidemic illness could cause in the form of deserted Indian villages left from the ravages of the second smallpox epidemic suffered by the Arikaras in 1803 and 1804. There was still squash and corn in the fields, unharvested. Cruzette, one of the better hunters on the expedition, killed a buffalo cow earlier that day. Dinner that evening was roasted buffalo accompanied with roasted squash and corn, followed by fruit. It is possible that the corn and squash were stewed in a kettle, but the meat would be spit-roasted over an open fire. It would have taken a lot of skill, even in the fall when the buffalo would carry the highest amount of body fat in their annual cycle, to control the cooking to a degree at which the meat would not dry out. Buffalo is very lean, which makes it a bit more difficult to cook without drying it out to shoe leather consistency, and the prevailing method of outdoor trail cooking was to cook things well done to avoid any incidents of digestive recklessness.

As the expedition entered the area of the upper Missouri where the Mandan tribe now lived, its men's thoughts were on where to build a camp to ride out the winter. The few fur traders and frontiersmen who had traveled this far west all spoke of the Mandan villages as a place where the locals were friendly and travelers were welcome to stay a while—like an interstate truck stop without the trucks.

In late October, the snow began to fall, and finding a place to camp became imperative for survival. A few days after it started to snow, several white men who knew the area well visited the expedition. It was on this day that Lewis and Clark hired René Jessaume as an interpreter and met Hugh McCracken of the North West Company and explorers François Antoine and Charles Mackenzie. No doubt, this trio wanted to learn more about President Jefferson's plans for a westward expansion that would divvy up the economic pie in a way that would no longer benefit the British or the French.

In November 1804, the captains met Toussaint Charbonneau, who was living among the Hidatsa with his two wives, who had been captured by one of the raiding parties the Hidatsa had carried out in 1800 on the Shoshone tribe. Sacagawea was sold to Charbonneau as a slave when she was only twelve years old. He married her shortly thereafter. Charbonneau, upon hearing the third-party account of what Captain Lewis had spoken about when addressing the Mandans, decided she might serve well as an interpreter, and Lewis and Clark, after discovering his wife was of the Shoshone tribe, felt she would be invaluable when they arrived in Shoshone territory.

The building of the huts for the camp was completed, but most importantly, the meat house (smokehouse) was finished on November 18, 1804. This gave the men a great advantage for surviving the winter because they now had a way to preserve the large quantities of meat the hunters were bringing in. On November 19, the hunters brought in thirty-two deer, twelve elk and a buffalo, so the completion of the smokehouse was quite timely. The locals also brought corn as gifts, which helped fortify the diets of the men who were consuming five to six thousand calories a day and were still hungry. Despite the copious amounts of protein consumed, it was all lean game.

Upon hearing that the expedition would stay near the Mandan village, the chief spoke to Captain Lewis to tell them they were sad to hear the party was moving north, but happy to know they would be staying for the winter. Chief Big White of the Mandan said, "If we eat, you shall eat; if we starve, then you must starve also." In effect, we are now all in this together.

The winter camp was built and completed on Christmas Eve. The captains requested they not receive visitors the following day so the men could celebrate the holiday without any outside distractions.

The Mandans quickly realized the expedition had the means and the skills to produce metal weapons. These weapons were approved on a case-by-case basis and became a significant solution to augmenting the food supply by accepting dried corn for blacksmithing services rendered.

On December 7, 1804, the expedition hunters killed eleven buffalo, and only the tongues were eaten, as this was the most desirable meat to the men. The rest went to the wolves. The temperature dropped to forty-five degrees below zero. Frostbite was now common among the men. Under the extreme temperatures, it is unbelievable how much these soldiers accomplished. The journals documented the daily activities well, and it is amazing how much social interaction took place in the camp.

The men celebrated New Year's Day 1805 with a firing of the cannon and a glass of whiskey from Captain Clark followed by one from Captain Lewis. A large part of the expedition left the fort and went to the village to play music and dance for the locals. On this day, Ordway made an interesting comment about bringing food from different lodges and different kinds of diets, signifying potluck had invaded cultures everywhere long ago and proving it wasn't invented by the Baptists like I was taught, but was certainly a genuine American custom. The tribe also gave the men presents of buffalo robes and some corn. This New Year's dinner would have been an interesting experience for these men in 1805 and undoubtedly the highlight of their day besides the glasses of whiskey.

The food supply was dwindling at the beginning of February, and the boats still frozen in the ice. It was easy to see they were going to be there for a while longer. They assembled a hunting party, and in ten days, they were able to kill forty deer, three buffalo bulls and nineteen elk. Captain Clark complained the animals were so meager they were hardly of service. Butchering that quantity of meat in those conditions had to be exhausting but bleakly rewarding by being an integral part of providing sustenance for your comrades.

Tying up all the loose ends so when spring arrived they could get on their way was the order of business, and solidifying the deal for Charbonneau and his wife to come along was one of those ends. The captains thought of the details, as only a formality, but it turned out that was not so. After an offer was made, it was flatly rejected due to the terms. Charbonneau would not agree to stand guard or perform general chores and wanted the ability to leave at any time should he not get along with the other men. A few days later, Charbonneau came to his senses and acquiesced to the demands of Lewis and Clark. He was hired despite some reservations due to his prior employment with the Hudson's Bay Company (HBC). Prior employment history was important even back then. Who knows why the quick change of heart? Maybe it was precipitated by the fact that Sacagawea had given birth to her son a few weeks earlier. Deciding to travel on the frontier with a newborn infant had to seem to some as a pretty crazy idea, but it is actually pretty crafty. Traveling the frontier with a woman and child sent the signal this was no war party, and that status would serve the expedition well in the near future.

As I stated earlier, the Mandan villages were a lot like an interstate highway truck stop when it came to information exchange and trading. In the following weeks, Lewis and Clark spoke to as many different tribes as they could. They were trying to ascertain as many different accounts of travel to the west and landmarks to find the river that led to the sea. Through fragmented and conflicting stories, somehow they gathered some pretty good information. Among the discoveries was the method of how the tribes made the colored beads. It was a secret held pretty close, and it was surprising to see it described in such great detail.

The boats are all finished now, and the keelboat and crew were ready to descend back to civilization. The weather was getting warmer every day but still freezing hard at night. Finally, around April 1, 1805, there was rain, thunder and hail, and the river rose. Clark recorded in the journal that they would depart with twenty-seven people and provisions for four months. It had to be sobering to write that entry knowing that in only 120 days, the supplies they needed to survive would be gone.

Chapter Five

Securing the American Fur Trade

This quote from Captain Lewis on April 7, 1805, truly puts into perspective his state of emotion at the time. It highlights the seriousness and joy under which they flung themselves so wholeheartedly and without any reservation into this endeavor. It also expresses the level of commitment expected from every member of the party:

> *Our vessels consisted of six small canoes, and two large perogues. This little fleet altho' not quite so rispectable* [sic] *as those of Columbus or Capt. Cook were* [sic] *still viewed by us with as much pleasure as those deservedly famed adventurers ever beheld theirs; and I dare say with quite as much anxiety for their safety and preservation. We were now about to penetrate a country at least two thousand miles in width, on which the foot of civillized* [sic] *man had never trodden; the good or evil it had in store for us was for experiment yet to determine, and these little vessells* [sic] *contained every article by which we were to expect to subsist or defend ourselves. However as this, the state of mind in which we are, generally gives the colouring to events, when the imagination* [sic] *is suffered to wander into futurity, the picture which now presented itself to me was a most pleasing one. Entertaining now as I do, the most confident hope of succeeding* [sic] *in a voyage which had formed a da*[r]*ling project of mine for the last ten years of my life, I could but esteem this moment of my our departure as among the most happy of my life. The party are in excellent health and sperits* [sic], *zealously attatched* [sic] *to the enterprise, and*

anxious to proceed; not a whisper of murmur or discontent to be heard among them, but all act in unison, and with the most perfect harmony.

This brief glimpse into the psyche of Meriwether Lewis displays the complexity of his emotions and the revelation that he probably did not know how to deal with those emotions as well as he would have liked.

The process of traveling upriver continued to go well. The crew was eager to go and cover as much ground (or river, as it were, in this case) as fast as they possibly could. This task became the focused intention of everyone involved. Walking on the shore looking for clues to unravel the mysteries of the local geography enabled the captain's discovery of some coal that they could use to make fires. They describe the view from the top of a bluff as the most delightful sight, and it is a very poetic passage:

The valley formed by the Missouri River was void of timber or underbrush exposing at a glance to the spectator immense herds of buffalo, elk, deer and antelopes feeding in one common and boundless pasture.

On April 25, their journey upriver brought them to the Yellowstone River. This description on May 2, 1805, of Clark's fondness for beaver is quite illuminating when taken into consideration on this day they acquired two deer, three elk and several buffalo; there was no lack for meat, so it must have been a flavor and texture thing.

Sent out some hunters who killed 2 deer 3 Elk and several buffaloe [sic]; *on our way this evening we also shot three beaver along the shore; these anamals* [sic] *in consequence of not being hunted are extreemly* [sic] *gentle, where they are hunted they never leave their lodges in the day, the flesh of the beaver is esteemed a delicacy* [sic] *among us; I think the tale a most delicious morsal* [sic], *when boiled it resembles in flavor the fresh tongues and sounds of the codfish, and is usually sufficiently large to afford a plentifull* [sic] *meal for two men.*

The reference to a resemblance of codfish is interesting and unusual, but it does not make me hungry for beaver tail. Maybe it would help if I had eaten only elk, buffalo and deer for a couple of years; then, probably anything different that would not kill you would be a welcoming change.

The journals reflect often that Sacagawea made a considerable contribution to the daily culinary offerings through her advanced foraging skills. These contributions are sprinkled throughout the journals in small mentions but appear regularly enough for another culinarian to realize she was sort of like the corps' produce purveyor. Gathering wild licorice and the breadroot (white apple), she provided the menu with many more variations. Captain Lewis made these observations about the root and managed to expound on its versatility.

This root forms a considerable article of food with the Indians of the Missouri, who for this purpose prepare them in several ways. They are esteemed good at all seasons of the year, but are best from the middle of July to the latter end of Autumn when they are sought and gathered by the provident part of the natives for their winter store. When collected they are striped [sic] of their rhind [sic] and strung on small throngs or chords [sic] and exposed to the sun or placed in the smoke of their fires to dry; when well dryed [sic] they will keep for several years, provided they are not permitted to become moist or damp; in this situation they usually pound them between two stones placed on a piece of parchment, untill they reduce it to a fine powder thus prepared they thicken their soupe with it; sometimes they also boil these dryed [sic] roots with their meat without breaking them; when green they are generally boiled with their meat, sometimes mashing them or otherwise as they think proper. They also prepare an agreeable dish with them by boiling and mashing them and adding the marrow grease of the buffaloe [sic] and some buries [sic], until the whole be of the consistency of a haisty [sic] pudding. They also eat this root roasted and frequently make hearty meals of it raw without sustaining any inconvenience or injury therefrom. The White or brown bear feed very much on this root, which their tallons [sic] assist them to procure very readily. The white apple appears to me to be a tastless [sic] insipid food of itself tho' I have no doubt but it is a very healthy and moderately nutricious [sic] food. I have no doubt but our epicures would admire this root very much, it would serve them in their ragouts and gravies instead of the truffles Morella.

There were some highlights on the expedition that, considering the circumstances, were accomplishments of legendary culinary feats. These heroic endeavors resulted in some fantastic feasts that fueled the men for many days to come. There was a huge welcoming change from their usual daily rations that happened on May 9, when Charbonneau decided to show off his culinary chops and French heritage by making boudin blanc from buffalo meat. This feat accomplished trailside is admirable and exhibits a formidable culinary spirit. The technique described in the journals is not exactly how most chefs make boudin blanc (white sausage). It would be interesting to know if they used the corn grinder to grind the meat. One can make it by pounding and chopping the meat, but the grinder would be faster. Charbonneau may have called it white sausage if the buffalo meat was from a young calf whose meat may have resembled veal or the name to him meant the technique more than the ingredients. Traditionally heated brandy and milk are also used. We know they had the brandy, and they might have harvested some milk from a buffalo cow. The result was obviously a huge success by the way Captain Lewis describes it in this passage, which is probably the most emotionally charged narrative about food consumed during the entire journey:

> *I also killed one buffaloe* [sic] *which proved to be the best meat, it was in tolerable order; we saved the best of the meat, and from the cow I killed we saved the necessary materials for making what our wrighthand* [sic] *cook Charbono calls the boudin blanc,* [poudingue] *and immediately set him about preparing them for supper; this white pudding we all esteem one of the greatest delacies* [sic] *of the forrest* [sic]*, it may not be amiss therefore to give it a place. About 6 feet of the lower extremity of the large gut of the Buffaloe* [sic] *is the first mosel* [sic] *that the cook makes love to, this he holds fast at one end with the right hand, while with the forefinger and thumb of the left he gently compresses it, and discharges what he says is not good to eat, but of which in the squel* [sic] *we get a moderate portion; the mustle* [sic] *lying underneath the shoulder blade next to the back, and filletes* [sic] *are next saught* [sic]*, these are needed up very fine with a good portion of kidney suit* [suet]*; to this composition is then added a just proportion of pepper and salt and a small quantity of flour; thus far advanced, our skilfull opporater* [sic] *C—o seizes his recepticle* [sic]*, which has never once touched the water, for that would intirely distroy* [sic] *the regular order of the whole procedure; you will not forget that the side you now see is that covered with a good coat of fat provided the anamal* [sic] *be in good order; the operator sceizes* [sic] *the recepticle* [sic] *I say, and tying it fast at one end turns it inwards and begins now with repeated evolutions of the hand and arm, and a brisk motion of the finger and thumb to put in what he says is bon pour manger; thus by stuffing and compressing he soon distends the recepticle* [sic] *to the utmost limmits* [sic] *of it's* [sic] *power of expansion, and in the course of the opperation* [sic] *the it's* [sic] *longitudinal progress it drives from the other end of the recepticle* [sic] *a much larger portion of the* [blank] *than was previously discharged by the finger and thumb of the left hand in a former*

part of the operation; thus when the sides of the recepticle [sic] are skilfully [sic] exchanged the outer for the inner, and all is compleatly [sic] filled with something good to eat, it is tyed [sic] at the other end, but not any cut off, for that would make the pattern too scant; it is then baptised in the missouri with two dips and a flirt, and bobbed into the kettle; from whence after it be well boiled it is taken and fryed [sic] with bears oil untill [sic] it becomes brown, when it is ready to esswage [sic] the pangs of a keen appetite or such as travelers in the wilderness are seldom at a loss for.

It is very apparent that those sausages were some good eating. Some of the previous day's wild licorice probably accompanied them and some boiled root bread. A couple of days later, there is a mention of the amount of sour cherries available and how the natives use these berries in a form that closely resembles today's fruit roll-ups, a method used by the Pacific Northwest tribes from centuries prior. Choke cherries and currants are mentioned to be abundant as well as aromatic herbs which have probably been available all along but not mentioned as they would not have been that rare of a discovery. Around mid-May, there are a couple of days where wounded bears cause a bit of excitement along with the near loss of the boat carrying all of the important merchandise that would secure the success of the expedition. Charbonneau lost control of the boat and panicked, quite nearly capsizing the craft. It might be worth mentioning here that Charbonneau's reason for panicking might be that he could not swim. In fact, several members on the expedition could not swim. It is perplexing that they would have begun the arduous journey that mostly traversed water routes with nonswimmers in the party. Some of the equipment and supplies on board were swept over, and Sacagawea quickly and coolly retrieved the lost articles. These events perpetrated what the captains referred to as an occasion to console and cheer the spirits of the men, so they indulged in a sip of grog and a gill of spirits. The grog referred to would have been a mixture of rum and water, and the spirits would have been straight liquor.

On May 25, Clark described at length the first specimen of the bighorn sheep the expedition had collected. Captain Clark viewed what he thinks is a large mountain range to the west but is not quite sure. The following day, Lewis first viewed the Rocky Mountains, so the captains became the first Americans to view the Rocky Mountains.

The expedition reached the mouth of the Marias River on June 3 and Camp Deposit is made. Here, the expedition makes a cache (a temporary storage pit) of supplies to recover on the return trip, stashing the blacksmith's

A sketch of a cashe used at selected locations during the Lewis and Clark journey. *Courtesy of Pamela Heiligenthal.*

bellow and several other heavy items along with some provisions. Lewis and Clark established a number of cashes at selected locations during their journey. The men dug carefully into the well-drained ground, removed the dirt to some distance (to leave no traces), lined the pit, placed items in it and sealed and concealed its narrow entry hole.

At this point, they are looking for the Great Falls of the Missouri River. This landmark will verify they are heading in the right direction to find the ocean. Cruzatte, who had the most experience on the Missouri, was convinced the falls lay to the north. Captains Lewis and Clark believed the falls to be in the south. The crew stated they would follow the captains anywhere, but Lewis and Clark feared the mission might fail if they chose the wrong direction. They sent parties in both directions to ascertain the correct route.

On June 5, with Lewis headed in one direction and Clark in another, the corps search for the Great Falls the Mandans had spoken of. Both parties had plenty to eat; although the northern exploration was eating buffalo, the southern exploration decided to harvest a few prairie dogs. Captain Lewis describes cooking them in an experimental manner (it would have been nice if he alluded to what the technique was), and the flesh was quite satisfactory. But they also had some fish to accompany the other protein.

The mentions of enjoying marrowbone feasts and the delicacy of buffalo hump are cited frequently during this period on the trail; however, bounty never lasts. The Corps of Discovery were soon to experience the fastidious situation that is the opposite of bounty. After a few days of searching both directions, Captain Lewis finally heard what he thinks is the roaring of a waterfall on June 13. After a few more steps toward the sound, he saw the unmistakable spray of water that a huge waterfall exhibits. A sight that must have been quite relieving as it signified the directions they received were accurate and that the Columbia River could not be too far away. This passage illuminated the array of emotions as they relate to food consumption expressed ever so eloquently—well, sort of—by Captain Lewis:

> My fare is really sumptuous this evening; buffaloe's [sic] humps, tongues and marrowbones, fine trout parched meal pepper and salt, and a good appetite; the last is not considered the least of the luxuries.

The fish preparation described is a standard to this day for sautéing freshwater fish—a little cornmeal, some salt and pepper, a hot cast iron pan and a little oil, and you are in business. The menu was nutritionally varied too—fish, meat and plenty of fresh fruit, as it is noted there was an abundance of gooseberries and yellow currants.

Once again, Captain Lewis mentions his duties as chief cook, and I think he has discovered why so many culinarians do what they do. Most say they cook because they love to, but in fact, I think that Captain Lewis has discovered the real reason—they cook because of the love they receive in return for providing sustenance. The treat made by Captain Lewis was a large suet dumpling made with rehydrated buffalo meat. This would have resembled the Southern dish of chicken and dumplings with beef or buffalo replacing the chicken. This dish is still enjoyed even today in England and Ireland—here is my version, inspired by *The Lewis and Clark Cookbook* by Leslie Mansfield.

Suet Dumpling and Stewed Buffalo
Serves six.

2 pounds bison sirloin roast cut into 1-inch cubes
¼ cup all-purpose flour
2 tablespoons olive oil
½ cup congac
2 tablespoons butter
¾ cup finely chopped and rendered pancetta
2 shallots, finely chopped
2 peeled carrots, sliced
2 teaspoons minced garlic
2 cups beef stock
2 cups dry Bordeaux wine
2 tablespoons minced fresh parsley
salt and pepper to taste

Suet Dumplings:
4 ounces suet
1 cup all-purpose flour
½ teaspoon kosher salt
½ cup cold water

Season the bison meat with salt and pepper, and lightly toss with the flour. In a large pot, heat the olive oil over medium-high heat. Add the meat and brown on all sides. Stir in the cognac, scraping up any browned bits, and simmer until almost all of the liquid has evaporated. Transfer the meat to a bowl and set aside.

Add the butter to the pot and reduce heat to medium. Add the pancetta and sauté until lightly browned. Add the shallots and carrots and sauté until tender. Add the garlic and sauté until fragrant. Return the meat and any accumulated juices to the pot. Stir in the beef stock, Bordeaux wine and parsley and bring to a simmer. Cover the pot, reduce the heat to medium low and simmer for two hours or until the meat is very tender.

For the suet dumplings: Place the suet in a food processor and mix until finely ground. Add the flour and salt, and pulse until well combined. With the processor still running, pour in the water in a thin stream. Pulse until the dough comes together in a ball. Shape the dumplings into golf-ball sized balls.

Add the dumplings to the simmering stew and turn them to coat in the sauce. Cover the pot and continue to cook an additional 25 minutes. Serve with pride.

A second cache is made on June 27 to lighten their load even more. I suspect that viewing the Rocky Mountains at a closer distance day by day perpetuated the desire to travel as light as possible. The eggs all in one basket theory is also a factor, as they would have guarded against losing everything in case the stash was discovered or destroyed by natural causes.

Another Fourth of July rolled around, and a feast is made. It consisted of bacon, beans, suet dumplings and buffalo, so they had no cause to covet the sumptuous feasts of their countrymen on that day. One other rather important event took place that evening, and that was the consumption of the last of the spirits, except a little saved for medicinal purposes. It was a memorable night with fiddle playing, dancing and merriment. Our country's recent liberation was celebrated in sincerity especially among these men.

Game and buffalo became scarce. But in mid-July, Lewis tried to cook buffalo (for the first time) Native American style. Lewis found it palatable. Game was getting scarce as they rose through the mountains, and Lewis complained in his journal that the men were so used to having fresh game every day that they were not conserving, making it necessary to hunt every day. If you live next door to a supermarket, you might suffer from this syndrome, too.

Sacagawea began to recognize landmarks that she remembered as her nation's land and the path over the Continental Divide to where her people would live in the summer. On July 28, they arrived at the exact point on the river where she was taken captive five years prior. Contact with the Shoshones, Sacagawea's tribe, was imminent. The possibility of succeeding in their mission and finding a way to the West Coast suddenly seemed possible in a way it could not have until that moment. The seriousness of the situation and the necessity for conservation set in when they ate the last of the pork and realize they have just a little flour and corn left. They needed to make contact with the tribe soon to be able to get to a place where they can survive. Amazingly, they had not seen a native since they left the Mandan villages. As they continued on, they started to see human footprints and attempted to track them. Once again, when the locals discovered the party as it moved through their territory, a fire was set to notify everyone upriver someone was coming. In the second week of August, Lewis saw a young Shoshone brave on horseback at a distance but could not make contact. The men are no longer wearing any clothing other than shirts and trousers made of buckskin, so their appearance could have resembled one of the Shoshone tribe's enemies.

Since the water is flowing west, the discovery of what Lewis thinks is the Columbia River happened as they cross the Continental Divide. The spring he drank from is actually the beginning of the Lemhi River. The captains and the crew continued to search for the Shoshone village and encountered some tribe members who had already alerted Chief Cameahwait and the village of the expedition's presence. He arrives with his warriors, who escort the expedition back to their village. They presented a feast with an abundance of berries of all kinds. Lewis described someone summoning him into his abode to sample antelope and salmon. He now knew he was getting closer to the West Coast, and he really loved how that salmon tasted. In the council with the tribe, Sacagawea was advised her parents were deceased but then realized that Cameahwait is her brother. From reading the journals, it is apparent the communication here is much better than with previous tribes because of the accuracy of translation. The following day there is nothing to eat. The natives are living off dried berry cakes and fresh berries. The expedition is down to only two pounds of flour. Captain Lewis instructs the cook to use a pound and make a pastry with berries. The chief exclaims it was one of the finest things he had ever eaten. The captains hire a guide to get them to the ocean. He is an elder tribesman named Old Toby. From here, it is all downhill—literally and figuratively.

Looming food shortages become apparent when the Corps killed its first deer while among the Shoshone. An enlightening scenario played out as the Shoshone returned from their hunt empty handed. Hearing one of the soldiers fire his weapon, the party's hunters rode full speed to the spot where the deer had been killed and started to ravish the raw carcass. Here Captain Lewis describes his assessment of the debauchery:

> *I really did not until now think that human nature ever presented itself in a shape so nearly allyed* [sic] *to the brute creation. I viewed these poor starved divils* [sic] *with pity and compassion.*

It is hard to believe that even with the deprivation of food, the tribe still exhibited such generous hospitality to the expedition upon first encountering them. Once again, the men implement the technique of weaving bushes into a makeshift net and deploy it into the river, harvesting 528 fish for themselves and the tribe. The hunters of the party may not have been more skilled as hunters than the Shoshone, but having firearms greatly increases your odds of obtaining prey. They successfully obtained game in addition to the fish. Ingratiating themselves to the tribe and having brought Sacagawea home, the captains find that Chief Cameahwait tries to accommodate all their requests. Just as he had done with all the other tribes when he first addressed them, Captain Lewis lays out the possibility of trading arms for pelts. This expedition's main mission was to expand the United States westward and possibly find an interior water route to the West Coast. There was however, an ulterior motive all along, and it was to eliminate the existing fur trade between the tribes trading to the French and English.

Interestingly enough, even after Sacagawea reunited with her tribe, she decided to continue with the expedition. There is a lot of speculation about why, and I surmise even Charbono probably did not really know the real reason. If your background includes two distinctively different cultures, you might have more insight into this situation than most. The tribes could be extremely prejudiced against other, tribes especially if they had been at war before. Once Sacagawea was captured, she lived five years among the Hidatsa. Her acceptance among her people would not be the same. Having married a white man and producing a child with him would have made her

A sketch made by William Clark in February 1806. It depicts what Clark labels a "white salmon trout," later known as a coho salmon (*Oncorhynchus kisutch*). *Courtesy of Pamela Heiligenthal.*

an outcast, affecting her status with the Shoshone tribe. The adventure she had been a part of was now her life and was probably the closest resemblance to having a family she would ever know.

The party packed up and headed for the Columbia River. Salmon were now available to such a degree that they easily caught them by simply gigging them, and deer were still in reasonable supply. The temperature varied wildly, creating some forty-degree mornings and ninety-two-degree highs in the afternoon as they moved through the mountains. Elevation and season change produced very low temperatures in the morning, dropping at times to less than twenty degrees. They were now exploring land that no other white man had ever seen. As their travels took them through the mountains, they were freezing and subsisting on pheasants and the last of their corn. The men were threatening to eat a colt.

On August 26, the expedition crossed into Oregon Country and was no longer on land held in the accepted jurisdiction of the United States. This area remained disputed for decades. They soon met the Salish tribe who they referred to as flatheads. The Shoshone described them as the flatheads because of the way they wore their hair, not that they practiced head deformity, which another tribe called the flatheads actually did. They were able to procure more horses from the Salishes. These people almost used horses as a currency because of their abundance and the ability to take them captive.

Progress became an arduous task with surmounting difficulties due to the weather, terrain and the lack of food. Hunger was nagging on all the men in mid-September. There was no game to be found except a pheasant here and there.

Sacagawea came through with her root foraging skills again, obtaining some vegetation for the men, who were becoming sick for lack of vegetation in their diets. They succumbed to eating a young colt and another one the next day before reaching the Nez Perce tribe where they could barter for some dried fish and some roots. They continued to eat the horses for a lack of any other protein other than the dried fish and small game. In late September, they first saw the method by which the natives made the camas bulb into a substance they could utilize for making bread. Private Ordway refers to the technique as ingenious and proficient at producing a very tasty product. Now because of frequent availability, they introduced crawfish to round out the daily meal along with other fish and ducks from time to time. Yeah, they used to eat crawdads other places besides Louisiana.

Despite the fact that dried fish, dogs and roots were available for purchase and fresh fish was there for the catching, the captains and crew were not happy with the daily rations. The devouring of the horses was not as drastic as it might seem because they planned to leave the horses with the Nez Perce tribe, hoping to pick them back up on the return trip. Starve or have one less horse for the return trip was probably a pretty easy decision. From here, the plan was to go by canoe the rest of the way. It seems a bit optimistic to think that this tribe would care for the horses and return them when the expedition returned. However, the lure of trading with the white man and receiving guns and other tools in return for the pelts of animals the tribe would eat anyway seemed advantageous to every tribe it was offered to. On September 10, 1805, Clark met three braves who were searching for another tribe, which had stolen some of their horses. When asked about the ocean, the young men mention their family was there last fall and they reside on the plain at the base of these mountains. From there, the ocean is only five sleeps away. The braves also mention there is a white man who lives there who has the same cloth that Lewis and Clark carry. This revelation must have excited the captains because they now knew how far away they were from the ocean. One day, they were traveling on thirty-nine horses. No, wait a minute, they ate another one, so it is thirty-eight horses. Then bam, it's ditch the horses and go back to water travel in canoes at the drop of a hat. Well, more like the dropping of a bunch of trees, a whole lot of whacking with some axes and then burning out and sealing the hulls. Without women and drinking, the only thing left is working, and these guys got a lot of working done.

In early October, they branded the horses and left them with the sons of the chief who accompanied the party down river. During the bartering of the day, the captains manage to procure some roots and dried fish. Also in the vein of trying to kick-start the future fur trade, they procure some elk and otter skins from the Nez Perce. The concept of heating rocks to achieve geothermic results presented itself on October 17, when salmon was cooked by adding hot rocks to a basket that held water. The Corps of Discovery now descended the Clearwater and Snake Rivers and finally came onto the Columbia River. Traveling with the current downriver, they progress almost fifty miles a day. They start to see items among the tribes that indicate these people have had contact with other white people. Seeing things like red cloth of European origin and copper kettles would have inspired the men to push on even harder. At this time on the Columbia, the salmon had spawned, leaving millions of dead fish rotting on the banks of the river. Having never heard of or seen anything like this, they had to wonder why all the fish were dead. This sight prompted the men to purchase forty dogs from the natives, being somewhat concerned that eating the fish from the locals may not be safe, and the bloating gas they had from the camas roots was almost unbearable.

The expedition sighted Mount Hood, Mount Adams and Mount Saint Helens within a couple of days of each other in mid-October. Captain Lewis and Clark had to know by now they were viewing the mountains Captain Vancouver and Gray wrote about when they viewed them from their ships in 1792. This meant they were no longer exploring areas where no white man had been before. As the crew moved downriver, the lack of wood for fires is a subject that is worth mentioning. I found it interesting that the expedition repeatedly dispersed judgments about the natives having a propensity for stealing, but whenever the expedition needed something, they did not think twice about just taking it. A good example would be the scaffolds the tribes had made to dry their fish on the Columbia. It is apparent it took a lot of hard work to gather the wood to make them, yet the crew took them and used them for firewood when needed. It seems a bit inexcusable that they would just burn them, especially when the corps took great offense if a native reached into their bag trying to pilfer a little tobacco. The tribe they were interacting with here was the Yakima, on the Columbia to the west of present-day Pasco, Washington.

The daily rations now consisted of dried salmon, fresh salmon, rabbits and grouse, which they were growing very fond of, along with the occasional dog purchased from the tribes. All along, I was wondering why they were not making wine or beer because they had plenty of berries and water. In this passage, they reveal they made beer by accident. On October 21, Captain Clark made the following statement:

> One of our party, J. Collins, presented us with some very good beer made of the pa-shi-co-quar - mash bread, which bread is the remains of what was laid in as a part of our stores of provisions, at the first Flatheads, or Chopunnish nation at the head of the Kooskooskee River, which, by being frequently wet, molded and soured.

Simple fermentation has been around for thousands of years and practiced in more remote areas than the Columbia River gorge. It is, however, highly doubtful that the art of fermentation had ever been carried out in such a haphazard mobile manner.

Progress toward the arrival on the coast was rapidly becoming a reality. Traffic was common on this part of the Columbia River despite the falls and the many sections of harrowing rapids. The natives used this nation's system of rivers much like we use our interstate highway today. With many people using the river, the expedition knew exactly where to put in to the riverbank and unload the important goods or, if it was going to be really rough, where they needed to completely exit the river and transport the canoes overland, otherwise known as portage. They knew this from watching the canoes pass them and later detour from the water from time to time when proceeding was beyond even the advanced skill of the members of the tribes who had worked this river their whole lives. After passing the long and short narrows of the Columbia, the weather is typical for the Pacific Northwest in November—rainy, cold and windy in a way that was detrimental to the spirit and senses. The spirits are revived and triumphant when the crew reaches the intersection of the Sandy River because this marks the farthest part upriver Vancouver's expedition in 1792 had previously reached.

Ocean in sight, they could hear the waves breaking at night. Clark quickly did the math and recorded 4,142 miles from the mouth of the Missouri River to the Pacific Ocean. At that moment, there had to be a moment of sober reality for Meriwether Lewis as he now realized he would have to report to President Jefferson there is no all-water route that they could utilize for commercial applications. Often the question comes up when examining this journey—why didn't Jefferson send a ship to meet the corps? As it turns out, there was a war in Italy in 1806, and most of our naval fleet was over there. Personally, I wonder why the captains did not seek out the white men the natives spoke of or assign a couple of the crew members to stay on the beach to watch for ships. Making a connection with a ship could have been a double-edged sword if the ship was not American. If it was British or Spanish, the expedition could have been in danger of an armed conflict. The locals also would not have wanted any changes in their current trading practices, seeing as how the corps had nothing of consequence to offer to them. There was a trading ship that passed right by the spot where the expedition had camped right before they headed to the southern side of the Columbia River to build Fort Clatsop, but the locals did not make either party aware of each other's presence because of the reasons previously stated.

For twenty-four days, the captains and crew survived at Point Ellice on the Washington side just north of the Columbia River facing the stormy Pacific Ocean head on with nonstop rain. After searching for a better location where fresh water and game to hunt would be available, it became apparent they needed to relocate to a spot to ride out the winter. After a few excursions to the north, they could not find a desirable location. The locals who kept visiting the men told them the south side of the river had more game, and after a few excursions to find a suitable location, they discovered the site that would soon become Fort Clatsop. On November 27, 1805, an important moment in Northwest history took place when the captains put the choice of where to locate the camp for the winter to a vote. It was the first issue ever voted on in the Pacific Northwest by nonindigenous people. Sacagawea voted to go south because she heard from the locals that they could find an abundance of Wapato root there. Lewis likes the south location because of its proximity to the location they chose to set up a salt production facility about fifteen miles down the coast near Tillamook Head. The southern location won the vote.

Established as a winter camp, the expedition landed at Fort Clatsop after several weeks of camping near the shore where the expedition found the conditions very inhospitable. Just like many tourists who come to our beaches for the first time, the crew and their boats were in constant danger from the driftwood. No one expects pieces of driftwood large enough to demolish a car in those beautiful waves crashing in front of you. The waves are intoxicating to watch but quite sobering when you have to run to keep yourself from a two-hundred-foot tree. There was one advantage being on the coast, and that was the access to crab, mussels and all the other seafood available in the estuaries and rivers near Fort Clatsop.

Construction of Fort Clatsop would begin early December. They completed the fort near the first of the year. Unlike the previous winter, the Mandan's social interaction with the locals was minimal. The expedition had very little left to trade for goods and the coastal tribes' bartering methods could be exhausting. Lewis and Clark could not (and would not) compete with the existing trade values perpetuated by the docked ships. During this period, to obtain a robe made from sea otter skins, they actually talked Sacagawea out of her waistband of blue beads. It was the only item the chief, who possessed the robe, was willing to accept in exchange.

Near the fourth Thursday of November, the crew feasted on sturgeon, mushrooms, deer, duck, Wapato roots (for starch) and cranberries. A pretty good Thanksgiving menu before the holiday actually took hold, and considering the circumstances, it was sumptuous fare. (Our country did not start celebrating Thanksgiving Day until the Lincoln administration.) The bad weather and lack of game persisted through November and into December. In late November, there is a recording in the journals that the crew ate several hawks and found them to be quite tasty. The men continue to be proficient hunters, although sometimes they did not return for days with any game. Game was so scarce at times that the hunting party subsisted on what they could kill before acquiring enough meat to supply the crew for a few days. One of the items of sustenance offered by the locals was whale blubber. Captain Lewis described it as being very similar to pork fat and, when cooked, had a flavor not unlike that of the dog or the beaver. The first salt the crew was able to produce arrived with the blubber and was a huge treat to the men who had been without salt for a while. This excerpt from Captain Lewis describes how much salt helped and how much any sustenance was appreciated:

> *Capt Clark declares it to be a mear* [sic] *matter of indifference with him whether he uses it or not; for myself I must confess I felt a considerable inconvenience from the want of it; the want of bread I consider as trivial*

*provided, I get fat meat, for as to the species of meat I am not very particular,
the flesh of the dog the horse and the wolf, having from habit become equally
familiar with any other, and I have learned to think that if the chord* [sic] *be sufficiently strong, which binds the soul and body together, it does not so
much matter about the materials which copose* [sic] *it.*

This list of animals will attest to the veracity of that statement by Captain
Lewis outlined by *The Natural History of the Lewis and Clark Expedition* from
Michigan State University Press:

Deer: 1,001
Elk: 375
Bison: 227
Antelope: 62
Big horned sheep: 35
Bears, grizzly: 43
Bears, black: 23
Beaver (shot or trapped): 113
Otter: 16
Geese and Brant: 104
Grouse (all species): 46
Turkeys: 9
Plovers: 48
Wolves (only one eaten): 18
Indian dogs (purchased and consumed): 190
Horses: 12

This list does not reflect all the creatures and plant species consumed. In
early spring before the start for home, the locals brought a half bushel of
candlefish from about forty miles up the Columbia River. Captain Lewis
lauded praise on this wonderful morsel of goodness, enjoying them more
than any lake fish he had ever consumed. They fire roasted the fish and
enjoyed them without any other preparation. The schedule of daily activities
continued toward planning to arrive at the Rocky Mountains when the snow
would be scarce enough to cross back over without delay. The timing was
imperative to ending this journey successfully.

When the Corps of Discovery arrived at the coast, the evolution of society
in the Pacific Northwest would change forever. The epidemic of diseases
brought by Western man all but decimated the indigenous population, and

in our ignorance to tolerate differences of opinion, the frontiersmen-turned-diplomats robbed those people of their true destiny. Who is to say their existence would have been fruitful and without difficulty; no civilizations have ever evolved without conflict. Conflict among the tribes also played a major role in reducing the populations of the Pacific Northwest tribes. Somehow, it seems plausible that without the intervention of the traders who preceded Lewis and Clark's arrival, these tribes' evolution would have continued unencumbered, except for the tragedies they brought on each other and the impending arrival of settlers. By no means am I trying to minimize the unconceivable importance of this expedition. President Jefferson's plan for western expansion was by far the most important American endeavor ever attempted and accomplished after the revolution. Yes, I am saying it was more important than the Civil War and, in many ways, helped shape the outcome of that conflict.

To imagine a small platoon size excursion would successfully be able to navigate such an expanse of uncharted territory through unimaginable geography with hostile inhabitants while only suffering one casualty among their crew is almost inconceivable. Without this expedition, who is to say if we would have been able to expand our nation in the manner we did. For all of us who call the Pacific Northwest home, it is doubtful that without the heroic and determined completion of Lewis and Clark's mission, we would be able to enjoy our lives as we do. For those of us who offer the hospitality of food and drink to all who will come to enjoy it here in the Pacific Northwest, there is a certain indebtedness we owe to the men of this great expedition.

Securing the fur trade for American trappers by claiming sovereignty over these lands required getting back to Washington, D.C., to report to President Jefferson. The Corps of Discovery left Fort Clatsop in March 1806, and by September 1806, the members were taking their fist sips of whiskey.

Chapter Six

Westward Expansion Begins as the Wagons Start to Roll

The Pacific Northwest would develop slowly in the first couple of decades after Lewis and Clark returned home. Almost as soon as the party returned joyously unscathed to St. Louis, trouble started in the Chesapeake Bay. Relations with Britain were strained and starting to disintegrate around 1807. These tensions were intensified by a practice of the British navy called impressments. The Napoleonic Wars prompted the Royal Navy to increase its fleet from 175 ships to 400, creating a demand for more sailors. Although Britain could staff its navy in peacetime, during wartime, merchant shipping and privateers competed for men with nautical experience. Britain did not recognize the right of a British subject to relinquish his status and would board ships of various nationalities to remove all British sailors by force. They would then press them into service, demanding they be of service as crew members on the navy's ships or face imprisonment or death. The United States offered asylum to British deserters because we believed they had the right to become U.S. citizens. In 1808, American Navy captain Isaac Chauncy investigated the issue and found that 58 percent of the sailors docked in New York City were recent immigrants and that the majority of those who came from the Royal Navy were actually Irish.

These tensions reached a boiling point on a hot summer night in Norfolk, Virginia, where sailors in port would come ashore and drink as sailors do. The fuse was lit when a Royal Navy deserter who had become a crewman on the USS *Chesapeake* ran into some British officers whom he disrespected in a most flagrant manner, otherwise known as talking trash. The Royal

Navy officers recognized this former Londoner named Jenkin Ratford as a deserter. Those officers quickly returned to their ship to inform the captain of the HMS *Leopold* of Ratford's whereabouts. The captain then decided to fire upon the USS *Chesapeake* killing three and wounding eighteen before boarding and seizing four crew members identified as Royal Navy deserters, setting in motion the events that led up to the war of 1812. England's war with Napoleon was paramount. It could not (and would not) allow American merchant ships to do business with the French. The American public was outraged and demanded action. President Jefferson attempted trade embargos against England to appease the outrage of U.S. citizens, but this backfired. Not being able to export to the country that was buying most of our goods at the time drew more ire from our citizens than a little loss of liberty and/or life for a few sailors who deserted the British Navy.

A few major events happened during the War of 1812 in the Pacific Northwest that are worth mentioning. Many people (including many Americans) are not aware that not long after building the White House in 1800, the English burned it down to the ground in 1814. Another common misunderstanding about our early American history is most people think the "Star-Spangled Banner" was written during the Revolutionary War. Francis Scott Key was actually aboard an English ship in the Baltimore harbor in 1814 witnessing an attack by British warships on Americans when he penned the tune.

Right about now, you are probably wondering what the hell does this have to do with Pacific Northwest food and wine history. The War of 1812 shaped the western borders. The war was being waged on three fronts: the East Coast, Gulf Coast and the Great Lakes' northern border. It was not an issue on the West Coast, but it became apparent that we needed to solidify our borders to the west and claim sovereignty over those lands for expansion. As the conflict grew in Washington, D.C., the city, including the White House, had to be evacuated.

Before the British invaded the newly built White House, President James Madison's wife, Dolley, iced down the best wines from the White House wine cellar and set them out for the troops. She had hoped our troops would be returning from the Battle of Bladensburg with her husband (our fourth president), President Madison. The president and a few American soldiers who stopped to quench their thirst before fleeing the city after they lost the Battle of Bladensburg drank some of the wine. Later that day, the British soldiers entered the city and consumed the rest of the wine before setting the White House ablaze. The war then moved to Baltimore where our military efforts gathered steam as evident by the lyrics of the "Star-Spangled Banner," written by Francis Scott Key while he watched the battle rage on from the hull of the HMS *Tonnant*, an English ship docked in the Baltimore Harbor.

Back in the Pacific Northwest, a major event in 1810 helped establish the first settlement in Oregon when the ship *Albatross* arrived on the Oregon coast after sailing from Boston. Captain Nathan Winship sailed forty miles upstream on the Columbia River to what was later named Oak Point. Here they started to build a house with the twenty-five Kanaka laborers they brought from Hawaii. By early June 1810, the timbers on the house reached ten feet high. The *Albatross* crew offloaded hogs and goats, began turning up the ground and planted vegetable seeds. This marked the first time a white man broke ground in Oregon. In mid-June, a party of Chinook and Chehalis Indians arrived. Although Captain Winship was wary of the locals, he had no idea they planned to capture the ship in an effort to thwart any competition with their centuries-old river trade route.

Upon realizing they would be under attack soon, the *Albatross* and its crew sailed back down the Columbia River to avoid what was sure to be a bloody massacre. But for this incident the Winship settlement would have been Oregon's "Jamestown."

Meanwhile, back at the mouth of the Columbia River only a mile or so from Lewis and Clark's Fort Clatsop, John Jacob Astor's company built Fort Astoria as a base of western operations for the Pacific Fur Company in 1811. Fort Astoria became the first American community on the Pacific Coast. This trading post was supposed to be a permanent American settlement completing the trade ring between New York and China with stops in Hawaii and Alaska. The Hawaii connection was to pick up produce and native laborers who eventually created their own village in the Fort Vancouver complex called Kanaka. As the War of 1812 raged on, the British forced Mr. Astor to relinquish control of Fort Astoria in 1813 to the British owned North West Company who controlled it for the next thirty-three years. It was renamed Fort George under British control.

Known for their hospitality, the North West Company men would keep the table full of food and whiskey. This was the life for the lucky frontiersmen on the few occasions when they came in from the wild. It was not so much the motive to build rapport but more to inebriate the sellers in an attempt to control negotiations. Here at this outpost, where drinking was probably an important source of entertainment, it is amazing how well some stories were recorded through oral histories. The one story that stood out was one about a seer who sought sanctuary at Fort Astoria, Kauxuma Nupika, a two-spirit woman who came to the post with her wife to seek refuge. After predicting a smallpox outbreak among a local tribe where she had been living, her presence became troublesome when the outbreak actually happened. The two-spirit designation is common among many Native American tribes and solidifies the fact that same-sex relationships are nothing new. This two-spirit woman and her wife created quite a stir and were probably a welcomed distraction from the bland diet of fish and vegetables that the outpost's visitors and administrators complained about. The boys at Fort Astoria thought the couple might be spies of the Hudson's Bay Company but were eager to befriend them due to their vast geographical knowledge of the interior. It seems there was a degree of social tolerance in the Pacific Northwest early on, but somehow, it went into hibernation leading up to the Civil War and remained locked away far beyond that conflict, especially when it came to race relations.

Obviously, from the complaints registered about the limited offerings of fish and indigenous plants, the trappers and traders had no appetite for the meat of the animals they were collecting pelts from—this fact was surprising, considering how the Corps of Discovery considered the flesh of the beaver a highly esteemed culinary offering preferring it to elk or buffalo. They obtained many of those pelts from local tribes, and it is probable they consumed most of the meat from the animals they trapped.

The locals had thinned the supply of deer and elk in the decade that passed between the time Lewis and Clark were there and when the maritime fur trade took hold. The lack of game for culinary use was much lamented by the inhabitants of Fort George and Fort Astoria, which seems odd for an enterprise where killing animals was part of the process. The pelts were primarily sea otter, fur seal, beaver and fox. Although Lewis and Clark's crew would consume almost any creature, apparently the Europeans were not that fond of the varmint-like critters. Fort Astoria would become the entry port for some of the first domestic livestock in 1814, when the British ship *Isaac Todd* left four Spanish cattle, some goats and some hogs. I reference this early shipment of livestock as some of the first because there are no references in history as to what happened to the goats and hogs left at the Winship settlement in 1810.

Oddly enough, although Astoria, Oregon, was named after John Jacob Astor, he was never actually there. The first member of the Astor family to finally venture west and see where a large part of their fortune was amassed was the first Baron Astor of Hever, who visited Astoria during the one-hundred-year celebration in 1911. I guess better late than never. John Jacob Astor would go on to become the richest man in America. From what history tells us, he would do it through a myriad of ventures that included purchasing the time left on the hundred-year lease for the island of Manhattan in 1804 (from then vice-president Aaron Burr) for a mere $62,500, thus becoming the landlord of Manhattan. That transaction enabled Mr. Astor to amass wealth at a rate never before achieved in America. With the War of 1812 disrupting his fur trade operations, Astor tried his hand at opium smuggling. In 1816, his American Fur Trading Company bought ten tons of Turkish opium and sold it in China. I use the term "tried his hand" loosely; it is very unlikely his hand ever touched a fur pelt much less the opium his company was smuggling. Most financial advisors, something Astor obviously took seriously, recommend diversification. This was probably not the first or the last of his smuggling operations. They just played a minor part in his rise to being America's first multimillionaire.

Other than the failed settlement at Oak point and Fort Astoria, outposts of trade and civilization did not exist in the Pacific Northwest until the conceptualization of Fort Vancouver. It was brilliantly brought to life through the joint efforts of the Hudson's Bay Company and the United Kingdom in the disputed land area called the Columbia District by the British and referred to by the Americans as Oregon Country. Planting a garden was one of the first things the Hudson's Bay Company did when it established Fort Vancouver. At its height, the garden had expanded to eight acres and provided produce and a large number of flowering plants, shrubs and fruit trees. This large gardening operation was symbolic of the power that the HBC exerted over the entire region and was representative of their agricultural enterprise.

There were two men whose efforts shaped and developed the West Coast fur trade: Sir George Simpson and Dr. John McLoughlin. We can credit both men for advancing the development or destruction, depending on whether you are considering the views of settlers or local tribes, of the Pacific Northwest to a degree that surpasses all others. Dr. John McLoughlin would become a prominent fixture in the Pacific Northwest, and despite objections by his superiors, he would also claim responsibility for the success of many American settlers. Dr. McLoughlin expressed his heartfelt sentiments for those who came to the Pacific Northwest best in the statement he made when trying to explain why he had chosen to ignore the wishes of his superiors who did not want Fort Vancouver to offer aid to the Americans:

> But what else could I do as a man having a spark of humanity in my
> nature? I did not invite the Americans to come. To be frank, I greatly

Right: Fort Vancouver.
Vancouver, Washington.
Courtesy of Pamela Heiligenthal.

Below: Watermelon in the
Fort Vancouver garden.
Vancouver, Washington.
Courtesy of Pamela Heiligenthal.

regretted their coming, but they did come, covered with the dust of travel, worn out by fatigue, hardships and dangers incident to a very long and perilous journey...The Bible tells me that if my enemy is hungry, I must feed him, if naked, I must clothe him, but these destitute men and helpless women and children were not my enemies, and I am sure that God does not want me to do more for my enemies than these.

As you can see, he was a very benevolent man whose hospitality ran to the core of his being. Regardless of orders and to the contrary from his superiors, he could not bring himself to turn people away because they were not British citizens. Dr. McLoughlin made and maintained his reputation through the mastery of native dialects and negotiating the merger of the North West Company with the Hudson's Bay Company. He was also known to set a very fine table, providing guests with the finest food and drink available to anyone in the Oregon Territory.

Fur trappers were the first inhabitants of the Pacific Northwest to start fermenting grapes. Fort Vancouver gets the credit for being the first place in Oregon Country where people planted wine grapes and started making their own wine. They used European *Vitis vinifera* vines planted by the Hudson's Bay Company at Fort Vancouver in 1825. It was also reported that French fur trappers had wine grapes growing in Walla Walla, Washington, around the same time. Developing trade at the outpost's setup by the North West Company, Pacific Fur Company and the Hudson's Bay Company was the impetus that would eventually lead to goods and services being provided for the clientele who would bring pelts for trade. These traders were almost all of European descent and enjoyed drinking wine and spirits. Sprits were available for purchase, as there was a distillery established at Fort Vancouver, but wine was harder to come by. So in the vein of the pioneering American do-it-yourself way, early inhabitants of Fort Vancouver grew their own grapes and made their own wine just like it was done in the old country. The few early European settlers arriving to start life in the New World still wanted some of the familiar trappings from the Old World locations they came from. These new settlers would also bring tools, culinary utensils, recipes and techniques that were specific to the regions they migrated from.

Upon reaching Fort Vancouver in 1836, Walla Walla Valley–bound Narcissa Whitman, wife of famed missionary Marcus Whitman, noted the presence of *Vitis vinifera* and wine at the fort. Employees of the Hudson's Bay Company were the first settlers in the Walla Walla Valley region to farm wine grapes in the 1830s. By 1859, A.B. Roberts established one of the first vineyard nurseries. It contained eighty varieties of grapes that were originally from Orleans, France. Shortly after, Philip Ritz planted a vineyard with twenty-one grape varieties near what is now Walla Walla, Washington. When gold was discovered in Idaho in 1870, Walla Walla became the supply post for miners who needed flour, sugar, tobacco, fruits, vegetables and, of course, wine. In 1871, Roberts advertised that he had fifty tons of grapes for sale. In today's market, that translates to 3,200 cases of finished wine.

Frank Orselli from Lucca, Italy, arrived as an infantryman at Fort Walla Walla in 1857 and settled here. He planted 180 acres of wine grapes The vineyards were located north of Main Street from Second to Ninth Avenue. Orselli also opened the California Bakery at Second and Main. Although it was called a bakery, it was more like a general store, selling wine, liquor, tobacco, groceries, fruits, vegetables and wine grapes. In 1876, he reported he made 2,500 gallons of wine and sold it at the bakery. By 1882, there were twenty-six saloons in Walla Walla serving locally made wines to a population of four thousand people. That's a lot of watering holes for not that many people.

The commercial wine enterprise as we know it now in the Pacific Northwest would take some time to come. In Europe, where wine had been around for thousands of years, distribution was still not carried out in a fashion equal to what we see today. It is worth mentioning that by 1820, many of the Bordeaux and Burgundy producers of France, whose names are revered to this day as the pinnacle of French wine producers, were already being served at many of the East Coast hotels on their restaurant menus. Hotels such as the Tremont offered French wines on their list. This property marked the advent of the first modern hotels in America; it was built in 1829 by the same architect who built the Astor Hotel in New York. Defining the term *modern* back then was saying that it was the first with running water to the kitchen and laundry with indoor bathrooms and bathtubs in the basement. Another hotel, named the American Hotel, located in Niagara Falls, New York, was selling bottles of Saint-Julien Bordeaux for $1.00 and Margaux Medoc Bordeaux for $1.25.

So while the first wagons had not yet started rolling west on the Oregon Trail, hotels with running water were being built on the East Coast, and the finest French Bordeaux and Burgundies were being served in their dining rooms.

Oregon City became the first incorporated city west of the Rockies in 1829, when Dr. John McLoughlin realized the falls on the Willamette River would be a great place for a mill. McLoughlin would not leave Fort Vancouver until 1836, but his continued support of American settlers put him in a bit of hot water with joint occupation ending. It was not the first time Dr. McLoughlin had been in trouble. In fact, long before he was appointed chief factor at

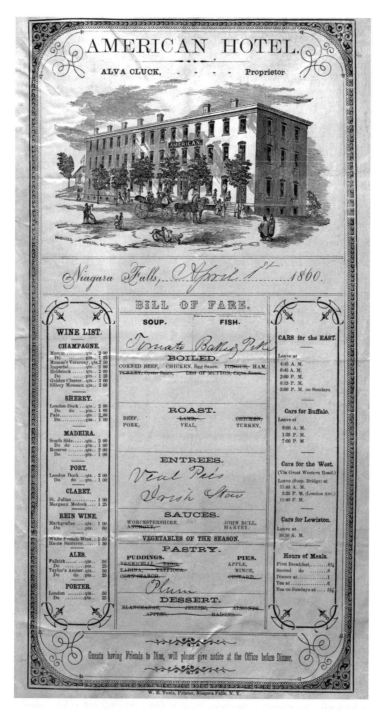

American Hotel menu. Saint-Julien and Margaux were sold for as little as one dollar a bottle. *Courtesy Hospitality Industry Archives.*

Fort Vancouver, he had been charged with committing murder. That life must have seemed a lifetime ago for a man who would eventually be called the father of Oregon Country. That did not stop him from becoming one of the most important figures in early Pacific Northwest history.

With three outposts established where settlers would be able to buy goods—Astoria on the coast, Fort Vancouver just up the mouth of the Columbia and Oregon City just a little way up the Willamette River—Oregon Country was poised to expand. All that was needed was the first wagon train to take the Oregon Trail. In the decades that followed Lewis and Clark's return from their famous expedition, the lure of the Northwest did not have a great appeal to anyone with good sense. At first, there were very few settlers making the trek west, and those who did were primarily involved in the fur trade. It was a very hard but lucrative life if you could develop the required skills. At the time, most men earned a dollar a day, and beaver pelts sold for four dollars. The demand for stovepipe hats made of beaver skin created an opportunity for wealth that attracted men such as famous explorer Jedediah Smith. Smith was an early follower of the Lewis and Clark expedition. Having read about it only a couple of years after its triumphant return, his desire to begin exploring was undoubtedly inspired by the unparalleled accomplishment achieved by Lewis and Clark. Jedediah made his way to St. Louis around 1826 and answered an advertisement seeking able-bodied young men who would commit to a commercial enterprise that would tax the spirit, energize the soul and lay waste to the body. (I'm not really sure they said it like that but it's probably pretty close.) Amazingly, there were plenty of hearty individuals crazy enough to say, "Sign me up!" It is reported that Smith returned from this expedition with four and a half tons of animal pelts—a record haul at this time.

The Pacific Northwest owes a debt of gratitude to Dr. Titus G.V. Simons, a name that never seems to come up when discussing the region's early influencers. Dr. Simons, known for being a tireless physician who provided care to the men who built the Erie Canal, was also responsible for giving Jedediah Smith a copy of Lewis and Clark's journal. Without reading that book, Jedediah would have never rediscovered the South Pass. John Astor's men discovered it in 1813 but kept it a secret.

This rediscovery was possible through the help Jedediah Smith received from the Crow Indians who lived in the Wind River Valley. While Smith was wintering with them in 1823, they made a map on a buffalo hide. On his expedition west in 1830, Smith returned to the Pacific Northwest with eighty-two men and ten wagons. That excursion became the first wagon train on the Oregon Trail.

Jedediah Smith crossing the burning Mojave Desert during the 1826 trek to California. *Courtesy of the Library of Congress Prints and Photographs Division Washington, D.C., 20540 U.S.A.*

The Oregon missionaries were the first nonexplorers to try and make a go of settling in the Pacific Northwest. Between 1830 and 1832, Hall J. Kelley attempted to found a colony in Oregon but failed, as did another leader, Nathaniel J. Wyeth, more notably famous for his advances in the ice industry, something he would return to when his efforts in Oregon did not work out. Not to be deterred, Wyeth tried again in 1834, but his settlements were not permanent. He returned to the East Coast and pioneered the concept of always being able to offer a guest a cold drink—certainly a noble cause. John Ball was a member of Wyeth's excursion to the Pacific Northwest. This excerpt from Ball's 1932 journal, *Across the Plains to Oregon*, illuminates the bounty that existed at Fort Vancouver and the generosity of Dr. McLoughlin:

The fur trade was their business, and if an American vessel came into the river or onto the coast for trade they would at once bid up on furs to a ruinous price— ten to one above their usual tariff. And as the voyage around Cape Horn from England was so long to bring supplies, they got a bull and seven or six cows from California and in seven years had about 400 cattle. They had turned the prairies into wheat fields and had much beyond their wants, ground by ox power and made good flour. Salmon was so abundant that the men would throw it away to get some old imported salt beef, for they had not yet killed any of their own raising. To show the climate, the wheat green all winter, for there was no snow, still spring and summer so cool that harvest did not come till last of July or August. Rained from middle of November till New Year's incessantly with the temperature day and night about 40 to 45 degrees, then rain and shine till May, frost, clear nights and vegetation nearly stationary, grass for the cattle, but cold for them out, the summer cool and dry, still the wheat first rate, the berry large and good, corn did not mature. Potatoes and vegetables seemed to do well, and were dug in winter as used.

A few fur traders and missionaries in service to Native Americans had better fortune than Nathaniel Wyeth, who founded Fort William and Fort Hall. Both were eventually sold to the Hudson's Bay Company. In 1840, most of the white men in Oregon Country were British fur traders. It was not until 1842 that the tide of American migration responded to the strong draw to Oregon. Within a few years, the Americans greatly outnumbered the British.

The discovery of the South Pass by Jedediah Smith was pivotal for the early settlement of the area. The South Pass made traversing the Rocky Mountains much easier and wagon trains became an American institution. The only other way was to take a ship from Portland, Maine, Boston, Massachusetts or New York around South America and hope you made it to the Northwest Pacific Coast. It was expensive and dangerous but nothing like taking off through the open prairie where bandits of every kind would take from you what you could not defend. Think about it: two thousand miles to cross, and it took four to six months to complete. This is almost two hundred days of traveling in what one might describe as dangerously vulnerable conditions. To compare the two choices, completing the trek to the Pacific Northwest on the Oregon Trail versus sailing to Astoria on a ship would be similar in comparison to someone who moves by renting a truck (packing it, driving it and unloading it) versus those privileged few who get to fly to where they are going, while all of their possessions are carefully unloaded and placed inside the residence. With very few people having the means to accomplish the water voyage, settlers trickled into the Pacific Northwest just a few at a time. Somehow, somewhere, something changed, and a light went off illuminating the bounty of the Northwest. The desire for starting a new life in a remote location suddenly appealed to people from all over our country. New immigrants landing in New England were not the only people coming down with "Oregon Fever." Folks from the South also found the Northwest Territory desirable. Midwesterners pulled up stakes and left their homesteads to avoid the crowding they felt when they left the eastern seaboard for the rural farm life of the midwestern river basins.

New generations of those settlers undoubtedly sought the excitement frontier life offered, and reports that wheat grew as tall as a man and turnips could grow to be almost five feet in diameter undoubtedly added fuel to the fire.

This excerpt from Lansford W. Hastings book, *Emigrants' Guide to Oregon and California*, describes recommendations for what settlers should bring for cooking on the Oregon Trail in 1840:

> *Very few cooking utensils, should be taken, as they very, much increase the load, to avoid which, is always a consideration of paramount importance. A baking-kettle, frying-pan, tea-kettle, tea-pot, and coffee-pot, are all the furniture of this kind that is essential, which, together with tin plates, tin cups, ordinary knives, forks, spoons, and a coffee-mill, should constitute the entire kitchen apparatus.*

The culinary culture of wagon-train cuisine (not to be confused with chuck-wagon cuisine) was created and developed as the Oregon Trail became popular, beginning with the Peoria party. The aforementioned chuck-wagon cuisine was a knockoff of the original Oregon Trail grub. Chuck wagon is a reference to the rolling commissary that traveled with cattle drives; it was invented after the Civil War. The chuck wagon would have been a bit more luxurious than the wagon train because it would have had a steady supply of dry goods and an inexhaustible supply of beef—a bit different from making a two thousand mile journey with minimal room for provisions.

One of the Peoria party's pioneers was referred to as a restaurateur for his occupation prior to departing for Oregon. The beginning of wagon-trail cuisine probably began with Ralph L. Kilbourne, a restaurant keeper in Peoria, Illinois, who made the entire journey to Oregon in 1839–40 with Amos Cook, Francis Fletcher and Joseph Holman. Having a good cook on the trail did not ensure success, but it couldn't hurt. As it turns out, Kilbourne was a shipbuilder, too—well, sort of. He helped build the *Star of Oregon*, a schooner that he sailed to San Francisco in 1841 to trade for cattle. The Peoria party was rife with problems arising out of a struggle for leadership, resulting in only ten of the original party of twenty-two making it to Oregon.

Hey, let's face it. All you really need to cook a fantastic meal anywhere is an open fire, some oil or fat and a flat metal surface or a grate. Hell, even hot rocks will work. Your menu choices quadruple with the addition of a pot to boil things and a Dutch oven for baking and braising. These are the things you need to cook a great meal anywhere, anytime—well, these and some stuff to cook, but these basic elements are still pretty important.

Chapter Seven
Oregon

Organic from the Start

You know the funny thing about food is most people do not think that much about it as long as it is around (unless they are bored or hungry). Too often on the Oregon Trail, the tales of tragedy revolved around piss-poor planning and preparation. Often hostile and violent clashes with local tribes, weather disasters or even leadership within the expedition created problems that contributed to the difficulties of completing the trail. But having food to eat was all about planning, surviving, enjoying and enduring, in that order.

Culinary masterpieces certainly would have happened, despite the fact that there are not too many stories about them. Just having something to eat, for the most part, was as good as could be expected. However, as sure as the fire burns hot and the midday sun brought appetites to be conquered, there would have been some culinarians of valor who searched for the wild onion bulbs, fresh sage leaf or aromatic rosemary bush to showcase the flavors of a tender, well-cooked antelope steak, freshly caught fish or the occasional roasted wild fowl. I do not doubt there was a good bottle of wine stashed here and there for the few who really enjoyed a meal. Why would anyone increase the weight of his load for something so fragile? Probably for the same reason many of us collect wines today: so we can have something nice to drink on a special occasion. Spirits would have been the beverage of choice, as they weighed the same as beer or wine but were ten to twenty times more potent. The added medical attributions made it an attractive staple. Many of the settlers who took the trail were teetotalers whose lips would never grace a drop of liquor. It would have certainly lightened the load in many more ways besides taking a load off the livestock.

If you arrived in Oregon Country between 1844 and 1845 and wanted an alcoholic beverage, you had to know someone with an active still, brewing or fermentation apparatus. Morton Matthew McCarver, who was elected speaker of the legislative committee in 1844, instituted a prohibition of the production of ardent spirits. McCarver felt that ardent spirits would bring withering ruin upon the community, hampering prosperity, and present a real danger if the local tribes could obtain them. Enforcing prohibition was next to impossible. There was only one marshal for the whole territory at the time, which would mean not many would be arrested for violating the prohibition. A year later, folks came to their senses, and the ban was lifted.

Who Took the Trail?

The Oregon Trail appealed to a very specific group of people. It did not appeal to the wealthy or the very poor. The wealthy had no reason to risk their status, and the very poor did not have the resources to purchase the needed supplies to make the trip. Much of what happened on the trail stayed on the trail because the mix of people who headed west was not too dissimilar to those who are drawn to Las Vegas. You know before you go. It's a gamble, and it might not work out in your favor. There is a pretty good chance it is probably better than where you came from, and if your luck holds out, you can change your life for the better. It won't be easy, and it probably won't be pretty. Depending on your circumstances, most likely, it will not be worse than where you were, unless you starve to death or the natives attack. Load it up, and roll it out. May your horses stay strong and luck be with you.

Before the advent of the electronic age (pre-telegraph) if you had problems like owing someone money, a warrant issued for your arrest or just needed a new start for whatever reason, you just moved. There were no credit-reporting agencies whose records followed you everywhere as they do today. If you went to the Pacific Northwest, chances were that no one would know you unless you were seriously notorious (like a picture on a wanted poster), and even then, if you made it all the way there, you would be in the company of similar individuals. The secret was to keep your nose clean and contribute to the community, and your new identity would be secure.

Commiserating the day-to-day activities of assaulting the olfactory senses by the excrement dropped from livestock as wagon wheels rolled across the dusty prairie has been told before. For the uninitiated, I am talking about experiencing the horrific smells of oxen, mule or equine bowel movements up close and tactile, like the occasional squirt of feces toward the unsuspecting inhabitants of the buckboard, not exactly a pleasant experience. Gross as it may sound, it was only a small detail compared to being the target of a braves' raiding party. Beguiling you with descriptions of the horrific attacks on settlers by local tribes is not pertinent to this story. That subject is certainly pertinent and deserves to have some attention, but not here and not now.

I have not regaled you with extensive recipes and techniques of wagon-trail culinary activity, as it is not relevant to what makes the food and wine in the Pacific Northwest today so exciting, so let's move on. The truth is that food happened. If you understand the lowbrow concept that is reflected on the bumper sticker that says, "S**T HAPPENS," you will understand the difficulties of food on the trail. Most anyone who has ever cooked before will admit cooking can be frustrating. I am sure that many travelers on the great migrations experienced the misery of waking up one morning to discover their last bit of meat had turned rancid or that the yeast in the dough they were raising overnight did not grow. Moments of disappointment like those have remained unchanged among culinarians for at least five thousand years. Figuring out how to use a product without any going to waste demands resourceful and decisive actions, and life on the trail certainly did not make it any easier. Let's just say you probably do not want to be standing near a cook whose plans on the Plains suddenly changed. The chef would have to complete breakfast by four in the morning so the wagons could be rolling at daybreak. A long eight hours later, the chef would serve the main meal at noon. Foodways on the Oregon Trail were challenging, rewarding and often overwhelming. No matter how overwhelming, food preparation on the trail would be good training for the challenges that would present themselves once the settlers arrived at their final destination.

When the migrations arrived at the mountains, it had to inspire all of those who had made it that far. Just the change in aromas would be welcoming along with the astonishing scenery. The knowledge you were getting closer to your destination also had to be inspirational. The first time you see the Rocky Mountains up close, in my experience, has always been a moment of reckoning. For most of those early travelers, unless they were from one of the mountainous regions of Europe, they were the largest mountains they had ever seen. Reaching the mountains also signaled the possibility of new subsistence options presenting themselves. Mushrooms (for the brave at heart and mind),

Breaking up Camp at Sunrise, by Alfred Jacob Miller. *Courtesy of Wikipedia.*

berries, fish and game must have inspired many new culinary creations. These new creations came from tried and true recipes with adaptations that substituted new ingredients. Such changes are always an exciting time for creative cooks. I'm sure the excitement was accentuated for those who ate the food those rolling kitchens prepared. For some of the lucky pioneers, bison would have been one of the proteins they would have at their disposal. This recipe for bubble and squeak is a classic using a newly discovered ingredient.

Bubble and Squeak

2 pounds bison
1 ounce bacon fat
2 cups cooked cabbage, chopped

Pan Sauce:
2 tablespoons bacon fat
2 tablespoons flour
1 cup beef stock

Mushroom ketchup:
1½ pounds mushrooms
1½ tablespoons pickling salt
2 bay leaves
3 cups water
1½ cups white wine vinegar
1 small onion, peeled
½ teaspoon grated nutmeg
½ teaspoon ground ginger
½ teaspoon pepper
¼ cup ardent spirits

Start by preparing the mushroom ketchup. Combine mushrooms, salt and bay leaves in a bowl. Cover and let sit overnight. Transfer the mushroom mixture to a cooking pot and add the remaining ingredients. Bring to a boil over medium-high heat. Then reduce heat and simmer until mixture gets thick. Remove from heat and cool. Strain the mixture with a piece of cloth, squeezing out all of the liquid.

Sauté the bison with bacon fat until it is golden brown. Add the cabbage and cook until heated through. Remove from pan. Prepare the sauce by adding bacon fat to the pan. Add the flour and stir. Add the beef stock and cook until thickened. Add 3 tablespoons mushroom ketchup and stir, then spoon over bison and cabbage and serve.

Here is another simple recipe for plum butter, as plums were readily available on the trail.

Plum Butter

Take a gallon of fresh plums and boil them with a half gallon of molasses. While stirring constantly, remove all pits. Keep boiling until smooth and thick. Store in airtight containers. Use on breads, pies and cakes. This recipe would also work well in sauces for pork and rabbit.

The last leg of the Oregon Trail as you emerged from the mountains would have evoked the light at the end of the tunnel response from the fortunate hardy pioneers who had succeeded this far. By the mid-1840s, the Marcus Whitman mission in Walla Walla was able to supply flour and vegetables to the immigrants arriving in their wagon trains often met miles away from the mission. This assistance encouraged settlers to persevere and carry on. However, celebrating success was a long way off for most. For some, it would prove to be unobtainable. The unrelenting pounding rapids of the Columbia River would dash the dreams of many. As their belongings crashed against the rocks and sunk to the bottom so did their aspirations. Another horrible tragedy a few Oregon Trail travelers experienced was getting lost in the Cascade Mountains never to be seen again. That scenario had to be the most egregious—to get so close and then to be denied the final reward.

The wagon-train migrations brought a sufficient amount of women and children into the Pacific Northwest to cause a major change in social structure. The system that had previously worked for pioneers and trappers would need improvements to accommodate families. The needs for schools and infrastructures to develop commercial enterprises were necessary. Ernest forthright husbands and fathers would need some type of governing body to make sure rights are respected, families are protected and laws are obeyed. This was to become the career calling for a mountain man and trapper called Joseph Meek. At the young age of twenty-eight, Meek had spent a decade living in the mountains trapping and hunting. The stovepipe hat that had been so popular was no longer at the height of fashion, and the beavers they were made from were becoming extinct. The lucrative life for trappers was on the wane due to lack of demand for beaver pelts. In 1840, Meek received a request from his old friend Robert Newell to join him at Fort Hall. It seemed a timely distraction and worthy endeavor. Upon arrival at Fort Hall, Newell convinced Meek the time had come to stop fighting Indians, wading into beaver dams or starving and freezing every winter. It was to be a gradual transformation for these rugged, lawless pioneers to become men who would eventually be the lawmakers and citizens charged with executing the laws of a newly formed territory. By 1843, Joseph Meek was an integral fixture in Oregon politics.

HOW DID OREGON BECOME A STATE?

The first attempt to form a government in Oregon Country arose out of the need to probate the estate of one of the first settlers, Ewing Young, an influential and wealthy man. When the endeavor ultimately failed to produce a government in 1941, Oregonians attempted again in 1843. The assembly of participants was quite an affair, and they commenced by voting in an open-air meeting at Champoeg on July 5, 1843, to establish Oregon's provisional government. Talk about putting the cart in front of the horse. The British held joint authority over the region with the Americans from 1812 until June 1846. With those facts in mind, one might wonder had the treaty gone the other way, whether the new inhabitants of Oregon Country would have acquiesced to British rule.

Only a few hundred non–Native Americans lived in Oregon Country at this time. It is plausible to wonder if the few who were chosen to make the laws had any idea that those laws would soon govern hundreds of thousands of people. What is now the State of Oregon was known as Champoeg back then, and what would become Washington State was called Clackcamas, but only for a short time.

In May 1844, an election was held for officers of the provisional government, at which some two hundred votes were cast, doubling the amount of voters from the 1843 ballot. Showing up to vote was becoming a popular social statement and a pretty good reason to indulge in a few libations.

The congregation for the vote on territorial legislation was a spirited group in more ways than one, as depicted in the portrait *Inception of Birth of Oregon* by Theodore Gegoux. Joseph Meek pictured in the forefront seems a bit more animated than the others do. Was it genuine enthusiasm or just good use of the hops, grains and the luxuriously pure water available in the Tuality plains? Meek was the very first elected law enforcement officer. He was made marshal of the territory. Joseph Meek also played an integral part in bringing the territory to statehood. A very outspoken and colorful man, he once responded to a federal official who was observing judicial proceedings about a case that involved a smuggler. When asked by that official, "What happened to the money that was confiscated?" Meek replied, "Money, what money? There was barely enough to split among the court officers." His dedication and allegiance to the territory never wavered despite the obvious forays into larcenous activities.

When I first read the Territorial Act, also called the Organic Act of 1848, my immediate thoughts were, "Wow, Oregon has been organic from the start." As a former chef who has worked in East Coast, West Coast and Chicago restaurants, I can personally attest to the fact that nowhere else in the country is the organic sustainable concept taken as seriously as it is here in the Pacific Northwest. Turns out the Organic Act of 1848 had nothing to do with how they farmed or raised their livestock. United States law describes an Organic Act as a decree from Congress that establishes a new territory of the United States or assigning an agency of the government to manage specific federal lands. No produce, dairy products or meat were involved, just dirt. However, Oregon dirt turned out to be, and still remains, some of the most fertile soil in the world.

The loosely formed government that eventually led the Oregon Territory to statehood was religiously and racially biased. The age-old Protestant vs. Catholic (Christian against Christian) conflict was the problem. The influence and interests of the Hudson's Bay Company, whose employees were primarily Catholic, was not in agreement with those of the Methodist missionaries who composed the other group. How any of them got into office is a mystery. Most had only been in Oregon Country for a short period. Samuel Thurston arrived in Oregon in 1847 after graduating from Dartmouth College and studying law under Ralph Dunlap, who had been the governor of Maine. Probably Dunlap's influence gave the young pioneer a propensity to become involved in government. Thurston was an ally of Jason Lee (the head of the Methodist missionary movement) and an associate of David Hill, the namesake for one of Willamette Valley's oldest wineries. Thurston settled in Hillsboro, where he practiced law. He joined the provisional government's legislative assembly in 1848, where he was elected as a U.S. congressional delegate the following year.

No one had more to do with settlers heading to Oregon than Samuel Thurston. He managed to convince congress in 1850 to approve the Donation Land Act. It would lure settlers from the eastern states to the Pacific Northwest with land grants. These grants were offering single men 320 acres and married couples 640 acres in the Oregon Territory. Those grants made the migration westward a lot more attractive, especially to young families. In fact, the marriage rate for those already in Oregon doubled for a short period. This was the first law of its kind in America in which women held property rights. The many tales of women and children on the Oregon Trail might have seemed out of place, but when the amount of land you could claim doubled, it became a promising opportunity for young families where the rewards outweighed the dangers.

The feud between the Protestant and Catholic factions in the territorial Northwest escalated to a national level when missionary Jason Lee and Samuel Thurston made false claims about Dr. John McLoughlin to the U.S. Supreme Court in an effort to have McLoughlin's homestead claims in Oregon City denied. Jason Lee and Samuel Thurston representing the Methodist's interests asserted that McLoughlin had sold plots of land from his homestead claim and amassed $200,000 from those sales.

Dr. McLoughlin's general store in Oregon City became famous and profitable as the last stop on the Oregon Trail. Just as it has been for thousands of years, sometimes someone's religious affiliations, which have absolutely nothing to do with commercial ventures, are a depiction to obtain undeserved power. These accusations were levied by Thurston who arrived in 1843 against Dr. McLoughlin who founded Fort Vancouver in 1826. In many circumstances, undeserved power was granted because of religion, but that was not the case in this instance.

In the end, McLoughlin did become a U.S. citizen but died with nothing to pass to his heirs despite being the man who made sure early settlers succeeded by providing credit for goods they needed. He did this with no discrimination regarding religion or consideration for country of origin. His dedication to his (Catholic) church, not his country (Canada, not Britain), among so many other blatantly unselfish attributes, earned this Irishman the moniker Father of the Oregon Country, and rightly so. Dr. John McLoughlin's posted and published admonishment to Thurston's accusations displayed here say it all:

He says that I have realized, up to the 4th of March, 1849, $200,000 from the sale of lots; this is wholly untrue. I have given away lots to the Methodists, Catholics, Presbyterians, Congregationalists and Baptists. I have given 8 lots to a Roman Catholic nunnery, 8 lots to the Clackamas Female Protestant Seminary, incorporated by the Oregon Legislature. The Trustees are all Protestants, although it is well known I am a Roman Catholic. In short, in one way and another I have donated to the county, to schools, to churches, and private individuals, more than three hundred town lots, and I never realized in cash $20,000 from all the original sales I have made. If I was an Englishman I see no reason *why I should not acknowledge it; but I am a Canadian by birth and an Irishman by descent. I declared my intention to become an American citizen on the 30th May, 1849, as any one may see who will examine the records of the court, in this place. Mr. Thurston knew this fact—he asked me for my vote and influence. Why did he ask me for my vote if I had not one to give? I voted and voted against him, as he well knew, and as he seems well to remember.*

Ironically, the two men who had the most to do with people immigrating to and surviving in the Pacific Northwest would become bitter enemies and facilitate each other's death, although somewhat indirectly, because neither man had an actual hand in the other's demise. Mr. Thurston succumbed to yellow fever while returning home to Oregon. Had he not traveled to Washington, D.C., to testify before the Supreme Court about Dr. McLoughlin's homestead claim, he most likely would not have contracted the yellow fever. In 1851, Thurston passed away at only thirty-five years of age. Six years later on September 3, 1857, Dr. McLoughlin died a broken-hearted man before concluding the land dispute and legal actions. He became an American citizen, and eventually, his heirs were compensated. But compared to what he had done for our country, we failed to do right by Dr. McLoughlin.

The single most important substance for human survival is water, and the Pacific Northwest has plenty of water. Fresh streams, lakes and, of course, the Pacific Ocean, which did not provide water for consumption but it did provide an endless source of salt, crustaceans and fish. Many new arrivals described water as the one constant luxury. For sustenance, one only had to look to the water when there was nothing else to eat. Anywhere there was water, there were fish to catch and eat. Foraging for greens, mushrooms and berries was just as easy, as long as they were in season. With fall being temperate, short winters and early springs meant no one would starve in the Pacific Northwest unless you were too fussy, too ignorant or just too lazy.

In 1837, Ewing Young was in Sacramento with Thomas J. Hubbard attempting to import more cattle to Oregon. They met a sheepherder named Lease, who they convinced to drive his herd of nine hundred sheep overland some five hundred miles to the north. Those sheep and the wool they provided started one of the early industries because of the costliness and scarcity of woolen fabrics. The first woolen mill opened in Salem, Oregon, in 1857 by Joseph Watt. Besides a thriving wool industry, the

Angora breed of goats and Willamette Valley hogs contributed substantially to the livestock successfully raised in the Pacific Northwest during the last half of the nineteenth century.

The migrations west continued, bringing the population to a substantial number, but it was the Whitman Mission massacre and the looming Civil War that hastened the federal decision to make Oregon the thirty-third state in the union. Oregon Country had now gone from being a territory where two nations shared joint occupation to a territory recognized by our nation as the thirty-third state in the Union on February 14, 1859, just ahead of the Civil War years. In only ten years, the population of new inhabitants in the Pacific Northwestern territory known as Oregon Country ballooned to almost ten thousand. These hearty individuals bravely staked their hopes and dreams on surviving in a place where few had gone before. By 1853, when Washington separated from the Oregon Territory, there were almost four thousand Washingtonian inhabitants. When Oregon became a state, prior to the start of the Civil War in 1859, the population exploded to a whopping fifty-two thousand, and Washington Territory could boast that almost twelve thousand people were calling it home. This was an increase of almost eight thousand new arrivals since 1853. That's a lot of hungry settlers, but fortunately for them, the bounty of the region was almost endless.

Down south, the California gold rush was transforming San Francisco into a bustling metropolis, complete with fine dining. For the epicureans who had found gold, there were but a few outlets to satisfy their desire for gastronomic pleasures. Sadly, the gold rush stifled the development of agriculture in California. The new wealth did, however, help to further the economic prosperity of Oregon, as it was the primary food source for many San Francisco restaurants. It only took a few years after the California gold rush played out before the Golden State's residents were maximizing the potential of that state's agricultural possibilities.

The progression of food in the Pacific Northwest is an incredible story. Where only a couple of decades earlier there was no livestock and no agricultural enterprise, suddenly things changed. There were thousands of acres of farmland and so much food grown that there was an excess to export. Wheat grew so well that they declared it currency. Merino wool from Willamette Valley was fetching a considerable price that was higher than wool from anywhere else and many were heralding Willamette Valley hogs as some of the best in the country. The bounty of Oregon also appealed to many Californians for whom the gold rush did not pan out and the first wave of immigrants started arriving from the south. Among them would be some of the first viticulturists bringing *Vitis vinifera* from cuttings in Lodi, Napa and Sonoma to southern Oregon. This would happen in the coming years, along with steam-powered ships, railroads and wars with the local tribes brought about by the discovery of gold.

Chapter Eight

The Early Days of Territorial Development and Cuisine

Before the joint occupancy of Oregon Country ended in 1846 and the British retreated to Canada, Puget Sound became a destination for newly arrived immigrants. They were determined to go only because the Hudson's Bay Company kept telling Americans not to go there. During the years between 1812 and 1846, the English sought to keep all American settlers south of the Columbia River just in case they could negotiate that divider as the border. They tried to discourage settlers from going north, with stories about fierce local tribes, poor farming conditions and terrible weather. The anti-English sentiment still ran deep, and Michael T. Simmons, a strong-willed Kentuckian, was one of the first who conspired to transpire against the Hudson's Bay Company. Simmons was convinced something up there was valuable and worth seeking out. He was already known to be unconventional, considering he traveled the Oregon Trail with a freed slave, something that would have raised a lot of eyebrows back then.

George W. Bush (Simmons's traveling partner) was an established and successful Missouri farmer looking to escape discrimination. When they arrived at Fort Vancouver, Bush had planned to settle in the Willamette Valley but found he was not welcome there. Simmons, Bush and three other families—the Joneses, McAllisters and Kindreds—would become the first five American families to settle in Puget Sound. Bush decided to make his home in Olympia on a fertile prairie that would eventually become known as Bush's Prairie. Bush built a reputation for providing food for all who needed it, whether they had money or not. His benevolence toward the Nisqually tribe, the regions first inhabitants, earned his family the knowledge of where to find and how to harvest the unfamiliar but bountiful seafood and indigenous vegetation of Puget Sound. Both Bush and Simmons became known as leaders in the community.

Simmons went on to found the Puget Sound Milling Company in August 1847 at the falls on the Deschutes River after two attempts at finding the right spot. Simmons first named it New Market to signify there was another merchant besides the Hudson's Bay Company outpost Fort Nisqually. He and his partners built the mill from equipment purchased from Fort Vancouver for a sum of $300, which was paid in lumber. They bargained for a price never seen before in the lumber business of $16 per thousand logs. It seems every product produced in the Pacific Northwest was fetching top dollar—wheat, merino wool, Willamette Valley hams and now lumber. In the following years, merchants began to populate the areas where these products were brought to market. This came about because of two things: these goods had to be picked up *and* paid for—wherever that was, there would be transportation so goods could be received and there would be people with money who were looking to buy things.

Things were starting to move fast in the Pacific Northwest now. All of a sudden, there were stagecoach lines, daily newspapers, merchants, bakeries, breweries and restaurants. Food establishments were starting to shift from "dining hall" status and slowly moving toward full-service restaurants. Nothing hastens an onslaught of merchants and merchandise like the discovery of gold. The first of these discoveries on the West Coast was Sutter's Mill in California near present day Coloma, California, in January 1848. Gold was later discovered in southern Oregon in 1850 near the Klamath Mountains. Both of those discoveries provided a steady need for all the goods and services that helped establish pre-statehood Oregon as the primary agricultural and livestock source on the West Coast.

To accurately discuss the history of Pacific Northwest food, it might help to first delineate where in the timeline of world food history progression we are. The two biggest disparities that should be contemplated would be what people of wealthy backgrounds ate and what the pioneering people who settled the Pacific Northwest ate. Undoubtedly, there were folks from both camps in residence in the Pacific Northwest during this time period, but wealthy individuals were not the majority. Knowledge of what the original inhabitants ate is a major contributor, especially as it relates to the organic locavore movement that defines our culinary culture today. There were no restaurants in America until the mid-nineteenth century except in major cities. The word itself was relatively new at that time. Few know that the word *restaurant* was derived from the word restore. In the beginning, the word was used by street vendors in Paris who offered restorative broths to improve one's health. This aspect of healthy eating was, in the beginning, a big attraction for taking a meal outside the home. But first, let's step back in time a little further to investigate the other attractions that gave rise to a cause for taking a meal outside one's domain.

Early records show evidence that establishments were serving food and drink in AD 79 in the ruins of Pompeii. Remarkably, there were over 150 food stalls located around the intersections of streets in the inner city. Prior to Mount Vesuvius erupting, there were around 35,000 inhabitants in the densely packed metropolitan area. With that many purveyors making food, it explains the curious lack of kitchens identified in the ruins in this ancient city. Each vendor's stall had an *L*-shaped counter with deep sunken wells that would hold cold or hot food. Also found in the ruins were saucepans, strainers, skillets and pastry cutters. It seems kitchenware has not changed much in twenty-one centuries. They had almost everything you would have today in a commercial kitchen. Pompeii had at least one commercial bakery, so bread would have been available for purchase in addition to beer, wine and other libations at one of the food stalls.

An *L*-shaped bar in Pompeii where food was served. *Courtesy of Wikipedia.*

A preserved bakery of Popidius Priscus, which includes an oven with large mills used to make flour. *Courtesy of Wikipedia.*

Long before France invented the word *restaurant*, Stephen H. West observed in his studies of the Chinese Song Dynasty in the early eleventh century that there was a direct relationship between the growth of early food vendors and institutions of entertainment such as theater, gambling and prostitution. All of these services were available to the expanding middle class during the Song Dynasty, and undoubtedly, their patrons were hungry and thirsty. In the northern capital city of Kaifeng, the population grew to more than one million people, and they developed one of the first paper currencies. The culture of hospitality encouraged the growth of teahouses and taverns. These were the first food establishments to cater to the needs of travelers. By the year AD 1275 near the end of the Song Dynasty, a written account notes the activities of street vendors in Hangzhou who prepared food to order, hot or cold. This excerpt taken from Mr. West's *Playing With Food: Performance, Food, and the Aesthetics of Artificiality in The Sung and Yuan* signifies something close to what we would call a restaurant was in operation:

> *The people of Hangzhou are very difficult to please. Hundreds of orders are given on all sides: this person wants something hot, another something cold, a third something tepid, a fourth something chilled; one wants cooked food, another raw, another chooses roast, another grill.*

This was pretty advanced compared to what was happening in the Pacific Northwest during the same time. No organized agriculture and a system of sustenance that did not mirror any capitalistic culture in any shape or form. If you walked up to the average person on the street and asked if he knew when restaurants were first created, you probably could not get an accurate answer. Most historians agree the first restaurants (as we know them today) were created around the time Thomas Jefferson went to France. This was just a mere circumstance—neither had anything to do with the other.

What a glorious time it would have been to arrive in France for anyone who had an interest in wine and food. Just as their custom still is today, the citizens were bursting at the seams to show how well they could make cheese, charcuterie, wine and anything else epicurean. Maybe I should qualify that statement by saying my definition of a restaurant is a location where individuals could sit at a private table and order from a list during set hours. The progression from food made and offered outside the home to food and drink offered from a list that one could order from while seated at a private table took almost two millennia AD 79 to AD 1782. Seven years before the French Revolution, there were a lot of changes happening in Paris. Antoine Beauvilliers opened the Grand Taverne de Londres in 1782. Many Parisians were enamored with the London lifestyle, and Beauvilliers capitalized on that by opening a London-style tavern that took food and wine service to the next level. This quote from the famous gastronome Jean-Anthelme Brillat-Savarin described what it was that made Beauvilliers so special: "[It was] the first to combine the four essentials: an elegant room, smart waiters, a choice cellar, and superior cooking."

During this same time, *service à la français* (service French style) was replaced by *service à la russe* (service Russian style), a manner of dining that involves courses brought to the table sequentially instead of the dining-hall style, where everything was placed on a table at once. It forms the basics of how all Western restaurants serve food today. In stark contrast to the culinary explosion that was happening in Europe, the original inhabitants of the Pacific Northwest evolved the patterns of their subsistence system for millennia without making any changes not dictated by environment or outside intervention. Pacific Northwest Native Americans brought a lot to the table in the way of new ingredients and cooking techniques compared to what was happening in other parts of the culinary universe in the eighteenth and nineteenth centuries. The food they made would have been and was considered simple by European standards. But was it? No. Not by any means—in fact, it is quite complex. Many of the staples that northwest tribes consumed took intricate knowledge of unique processing techniques to render those products for safe consumption. Here in the Pacific Northwest, tribal subsistence had developed from what was available just like tribes from all other regions across the Americas.

A good example of a simple dish that inquired intricate knowledge would be making acorn flour. It sounds easy: just gather some fallen nuts, grind them up and then use the flour to make bread. Try it using just these steps, and you may never eat acorn bread again. To eat acorns, you have to to leach the poisonous tannic acid that is part of their natural composition. This is a labor-intensive process to make them edible. Nutritional analysis of uncooked acorn meal shows that it is 21 percent fat, 5 percent protein, 62 percent carbohydrate and 14 percent water, mineral and fiber. With those numbers, it is easy to see how the carbohydrate and some of the protein needs of Northwest natives were being met. After carefully drying and crushing the acorns into a coarse meal, a popular preparation for natives and settlers alike would have been this recipe for acorn and berry cakes. What is needed is one roaring campfire and a Dutch oven or flat rock for cooking.

Acorn and Berry Cakes

1 cup acorn meal
½ cup cornmeal
1 cup fresh berries or nuts (whatever could be found)
1 teaspoon pearl ash
1 teaspoon salt
2 teaspoons sugar
1½ cups boiling water
Beef tallow or lard for frying

Place oven or flat rock on fire. If using a rock, make sure it is firmly situated and level. Mix flours, salt, berries and pearl ash in a container. Pour ½ cup of water into container and blend until mixture comes together. Continue adding water until a batter reaches a consistency that will form cakes when dropped onto a greased hot rock or Dutch oven. Cook until bubbles form. Then flip, and cook other side until done. Serve with butter and molasses (if available).

Another food staple of Northwest tribes that is still in existence and sold in supermarkets all over the world is dried fruit roll-ups. It is notable that this food item has remained virtually unchanged from ancient times to the present. The local tribes dried and ate many different types of fruits in the winter, mostly wild berries such as strawberries, blueberries, wild grapes, huckleberries, serviceberries, currants, cranberries and chokecherries. They would pound them with seeds intact and then dry them in the sun before stacking and storing them. For many of these tribes, chokecherry was the most important fruit in their diets. They would harvest the fruit when they were dark purple-black in color with no hint of red. Placing the fruit on large screens covered with muslin, the fruit would dry in hot weather for around four to five days. Each night, the chokecherries would go in an airtight container stored in a cool place to prevent spoilage until the next drying day.

One of the traditional Indian recipes that the tribes have passed through generations is wasna, with *wa* meaning "anything" and *sna* meaning "ground up." Most refer to it as pemmican. This dish consists of dried buffalo, dried berries and some sort of fat. The following is a traditional recipe that incorporates chokecherries.

Wasna (Pemmican)

1 pound unseasoned, dried buffalo
½ pound chokecherries
1 cup kidney fat or lard
2 cups sugar

Place the meat in a pillowcase and pound until fine with a hammer. Then, place the meat in a bowl and mix in the chokecherries and sugar. Heat the kidney fat (or lard) until melted. Cool until you can handle it with your hands, and then pour enough fat into the meat mixture to moisten and mix well. The mixture should stick together to make it easy for eating. Eat with a spoon or pinched into the hand.

Unlike European settlers who came here with what they were used to eating and tried to make it grow or find someone they could buy it from, native inhabitants operated in a different manner. In their society, commerce had not taken the path of individualistic capitalism that took hold in the eastern hemisphere. If you showed up to a tribe's village and they did not kill you, they would feed you. If they had food, they may ask for something in exchange, which shows substantial evidence that hospitality was a common trait among many Native American tribes, especially in the Pacific Northwest.

For the Pacific Northwest tribes in the nineteenth century, that was all about to change. Smallpox and other devastating illnesses decimated the Pacific Northwest tribes by as much as 90 percent between the years of 1840 and 1850. No matter how advanced any civilization may be, time after time, humanity has greeted others who seem similar without the consideration of unseen maladies, often with the same devastating results.

Chapter Nine

The First Californian Invasion

Planning in the early days of territorial cuisine required a calculated approach to dealing with many different variables. Those variables included making sure you did not have to eat raccoon, but if you did have to, it meant knowing how to cook one. People who planned well when they pioneered into the Pacific Northwest usually prospered well. Then again, as always, some people just fall ass backward into money.

Two Oregon pioneers whose adequate planning proved to be quite profitable were Henderson Luelling and William Meek. Luelling had the foresight after hearing about the fertile land of the Willamette Valley to load up two wagons full of fruit trees and wine-grape cuttings and head out on the Oregon Trail. Almost all the early fruit trees in Oregon were planted from the stock he and William Meek brought in 1847. Luelling planted his wine grapes on arrival, and by 1859, he was entering and winning competitions held at the California State Fair. Meek moved to Alameda County, California, and in 1874, the *Oregonian* newspaper reported he had 2,200 acres under cultivation, the largest in the state at the time. Luelling was quite a visionary. He saw orchards where there were none and European quality wine available for anyone's dinner table that desired it. Through his careful planning and perseverance, he made sure they would and could come to fruition.

The symbiotic relationship Oregon has with California presented itself often in the mid-nineteenth century. Swapping places between being a place where most of Oregon's livestock came from in the beginning to Oregon's agricultural bounty feeding San Francisco's early residents at the beginning of the gold rush, it was a give-and-take relationship.

The tale about the discovery of gold in Oregon is another example of that relationship. John R. Poole and James Cluggage were two guys who took advantage of the logistics quandary the discoveries of gold presented when those discoveries spread northward in California and finally to Siskiyou County, the northernmost point in that state. Taking supplies from Portland to Crescent City via waterways and then inland was expensive and time consuming. Poole and Cluggage created "Jackass Freight" a two-man pack-mule operation. Their little mule-powered supply train traversed the inland route over the Siskiyou Pass and into California. Poole and Cluggage made their final trip on this route in 1851. On that trip, they stopped to water the mules, perhaps before they fell backward. They decided to camp for the night in a location where the town of Jacksonville sits today. Needing to water the livestock, they started scraping out a hole near a gulch to fill with water. They looked down and much to their amazement, noticed placer gold in a significant quantity, bolstering the fact that sometimes asses just fall into money. Poole and Cluggage filed claims on several hundred acres and started laying out plans to build a town. A year later, just like magic, a town appeared, complete with two thousand inhabitants. Poole and Cluggage already knew mining gold was not for them because there was a lot more money in catering to the needs of those who mined. There was even more money to be made if you sold the things wanted and needed by those who found the gold. It seems gold was a great motivator for statesmen too. Other than the Whitman incident, it was the discovery of gold that took the Northwest from being a territory to statehood, complete with newspapers, lawyers, bankers, hotels, restaurants and wine and spirits producers. The correlation of the timing between the California gold rush and California's statehood being granted and Oregon's similar outcome could be coincidence with a big emphasis on the word *could*.

A year after Poole and Cluggage fell ass backward into money and created a city where there was none, one of the most prolific figures in the history of photography, Peter Britt, arrived in Jacksonville, Oregon. In 1852, he was traveling on foot with a small cart hauling his photography apparatus. It turns out the small cart was actually a half wagon. It was a whole wagon for 1,800 miles on the Oregon Trail. Somehow, when the wagon train reached the Grand Ronde Valley, other members of the wagon train would no longer deal with the three hundred pounds of photography equipment and cut it in half. Britt got the half without the buckboard. Once he made it to Portland, word of the gold discovery in Table Rock fueled the gold fever inside him, and with an ox, a mule and five dollars in his pocket, he walked to Jacksonville. In the field of photography, Britt was a luminary. He also was one of the earliest vintners in the state. Long before he established Oregon's first winery, Valley View Vineyard, Peter Britt grew grapes and sold wine in Jacksonville. Britt got his first grape cuttings from an Italian peddler from California in 1854, as did many southern Oregon viticulturists, including the Von Pessel's and A. Doerner, establishing the significance of what I call the "First California Invasion" in the history of Oregon wine. Peter Britt's own diary indicated that by 1870, he had experimented with over two hundred grape varieties. It would seem odd that Pinot noir, the famous grape of the Burgundy region in France, would not have been one of them. Contrary to the claim by many that there was no Oregon wine industry prior to Prohibition, by 1880, Britt was producing as much as three thousand gallons of wine a year, filling orders under his Valley View Vineyard label from as far away as Wyoming.

On September 11, 1899, the Yakima *Ranch and Range* newspaper reported that in Tacoma, Washington, Mr. J.E. Baker, another viticulturist and the State of Washington's horticultural commissioner, was quietly producing thousands of gallons of wine a year from grapes he grew or purchased from his neighbors and was selling it without a license or paying any taxes. Baker started by saying he had been doing this for the last thirty years. The column was printed to clarify a tax question an individual from Chelan had previously asked that was answered incorrectly by an IRS field agent. Baker stated in his rebuttal that "the question and answer as published was misleading and will have a tendency to injure one of the rapidly growing industries of the state the growing of grapes and other fruits and the making of wine there from." It seems Washingtonians had a commercial wine industry, according to Commissioner Baker, throughout the latter half of the nineteenth century.

Early Northwest settlers and travelers in search of fortune or farmland only had to look as far as the *Table Rock Sentinel* published in Jacksonville, Oregon. This publication offered anyone who had an inquiring mind to open the page and see multiple advertisements for hotels, restaurants and bakeries, all of which sold a good assortment of distilled spirits, wines and fresh beer. One such merchant was Mr. J.B. Truchot, who had a bakery on California Street— and not just any bakery, but a French bakery. Truchot also offered Champagne, claret, cognac, port and Sauternes. This merchant was one of the first of his kind to openly advertise a selection of superior French sweet white wine and other fine liquors for the ladies.

The *Sentinel* was only published between 1858 (a year before Oregon became a state) and 1888 (a year before Washington became a state). These three decades brought immense change to the Northwest. If the rest of the world had been aware of the speed at which this nation expanded westward, it would have been afraid of us, and rightly so. We also should have recognized the need to fear ourselves. Depletion and careless stewarding accompanied the prevailing bravado of development as the irony of idiots—otherwise known as beginner's luck—progressed forward, lurching toward civilization. Without the abundance of all the resources that constitute material wealth, the Pacific Northwest expansion would have fizzled and failed. Almost as abundant as the resources was the veracity of spirit expressed in the everyday endeavors of the common man. Staying the course and carrying out your actions in those untamed locations demanded determination. Along with being doggedly determined, it took the will to commit and, once committed, the endurance to see it through no matter what the undertaking was.

One such memorable occasion happened in 1852 when a ship docked in Crescent City, California. The ship's crew heard about the discovery of gold in the Rogue River Valley and jumped ship. The crew then made its way across the mountains and commenced prospecting near the old mining camp at Waldo, Oregon. Here the crew members struck "pay dirt" and discovered enough gold to attract many others for years to come, and all who came in search for the gold called it Sailors' Diggins. Another notable incident, which took place at Sailors' Diggins, was one of the worst Wild West killing rampages on record and a legendary tale of lost gold. In 1852, the Triskett Gang, a group of Oregon robbers on the run from a California posse after stealing some miners' gold down there, descended on the small town. Most of the men of the town were out mining gold when the gang arrived at the saloon and drank themselves into a stupor. Realizing they needed to get the hell out of there before the posse arrived, they were leaving when one of the gang snapped and shot a man who was walking down the street. The other four gang members then joined in and killed everyone on the street. The seventeen victims were mostly women, children and elderly residents. In a moment of larcenous clarity, the men decided to collect all the gold at the assayer's office, about 250 pounds, before they took off. The miners, hearing the shots, headed back to town to find the unsettling carnage, and in moments, they were chasing the bandits. Catching up to them quickly, the Triskett Gang's final stand was not a long-lived event, and when it was all over, none of the Triskett Gang was left alive. Somehow, the gold was never found. Today, it would be valued at more than $5 million. As you can imagine, for years after the incident, there would be many who would come in search of that gold. To this day, it has never been found.

Just like in California, the gold in Oregon eventually played out. Gold did make Walla Walla the biggest town in Washington from 1850 to 1860, but no gold was ever discovered there. It was just the closest civilization to where it was discovered in Idaho. The next gold discovery happened in Canada on the Frasier River in 1858. That discovery created another boomtown in Whatcom County, Washington, and started a rivalry about which city would become the dominate seaport on Puget Sound—Seattle or Bellingham. Although Bellingham is a fine city, I think by now we know Seattle won. Bellingham Bay became the overland starting point for those miners from California and Oregon who were headed north to the Canadian Frasier River strike to try their luck there. If you were Bellingham bound in those days, you might want to be on the lookout for and steer clear of Dirty Dan Harris of Fairhaven, Washington. Dan was a notorious smuggler, known to sell liquor to Native Americans, and a devious businessman, who traveled to the far points of the world before he was two decades old and saw almost everything there was to see, including setting foot in Antarctica while serving as a crewman aboard the *Levant* in 1853. Despite Dan's dubious dealings, the man gained social stature and amassed a fortune, even rising to a level where he made loans to a former California governor. His legend lives on to this day. In the city of Fairhaven on the site where he claimed his original Donation Land Grant, there is a restaurant named Dirty Dan Harris. Another early saloon of historical significance is the Horseshoe, which opened in Bellingham in 1886. Still open today and a favorite of Western Washington University students when they want to get their munch on, the Shoe, as they call, it is the oldest continuously operating twenty-four-hour restaurant west of the Mississippi River. The Horseshoe has been the place for a refreshing libation for almost as long as it has been in operation. It makes a chicken-fried steak with country gravy that is one of the best I've tasted this side of the Cascades. If you would like to re-create it, here is the recipe, compliments of the Horseshoe. I suggest you enjoy it with a glass of Washington Cabernet Sauvignon.

> ## Horseshoe Chicken-Fried Steak
>
> *Cube Steak: Combine eggs, buttermilk, salt and pepper in one bowl. Fill a shallow dish with flour. Dip cube steak in flour, then the egg mixture and then back in the flour. Fry steak until it reaches at least 145 degrees. Top with Country Gravy.*
>
> *Country Gravy: Combine onion, Tobasco, salt and pepper with ground country sausage. Cook until well browned. Add ham base and flour, stirring until well blended. Add equal parts milk and half and half. Cook until it reaches 160 degrees, stirring frequently. Add roux until you reach the thickness you desire.*

TRANSPORTATION CHANGES EVERYTHING

Transportation progress would change everything, and it started early on the Columbia River. By 1835, there were steamships operating in the Pacific Northwest, first on the Columbia River between Astoria and Fort Vancouver and then at Fort Nisqually in Puget Sound. Twenty-five years later, dozens of ships were ferrying passengers from Tacoma to Seattle and anywhere else on Puget Sound where commerce could be convened. As steam power advanced and wheat growth from the Columbia Valley expanded to direct exportation to Europe, wealth was spreading quickly on the Columbia River. Northwest river travel to Wallula (the closest river town to Walla Walla) was made possible in 1858 by short railroad portages at Celio Falls. A connecting intercontinental railroad arrived in 1883, connecting the Pacific Northwest to the rest of the country.

Comprehending the potential of what would and could happen in this uniquely beautiful place, Professor W.D. Lyman summed it up better than anyone from this time ever could when, in 1901, he wrote this assessment of how transportation was destined to change the Pacific Northwest:

> *Far seeing men like Whitman and others, even in the earliest period of settlement, plainly grasped the conception of the great steamboat lines along the rivers and the railroad lines across the praries [sic] and through the mountain passes, which would sometime bring that majestic wilderness into communication with the rest of the world.*

All of the glorious aspects of the Pacific Northwest that make it the pinnacle of wine and food destinations that it is today hinged on the progression of transportation. What does seem odd is that there were steamships and railroads before the daily stagecoach began. Daily stagecoach runs were dependent on overland routes. Continuing advances in transportation brought a daily stagecoach that ran from Portland to Sacramento in 1867. One traveler, Richard Erdoes, shared his observations in *Saloons of the Old West* about Pacific Northwest dining manners and the food served on the stagecoach lines in this brief observation:

> *Table manners were atrocious by European standards. Food was wolfed down with a speed that astounded the foreigner. At saloons that were also stagecoach stations, with only a limited time available for a stopover, it was every man for himself. A run was made for the table set out smorgasbord fashion, guests elbowing and trampling each other, devouring everything in sight in record time...Things were no different on the northwest coast: "They breakfast in the middle of the night, dine when they aught to be breakfasting and take supper when they should be dining; and the 'feed' is most distasteful—all noise, dirt, grease, mess, slop, confusion, and disorder; chunks of meat of all kinds and no flavor, placed in plates, and 'sot' on the table; and before you have time to look at your meat, a piece of very flat pie, with a doughy crust, and dried fruit inside is placed under your nose, on the same plate with your meat. Men pick their teeth with forks and jackknives, gobble down gallons of water, and 'slide.' This is the style in Oregon."*

Along with the modernization of transportation came the near extinction of the salmon on the Columbia River. Progress, as some might call it, always has its price. When I first came to the Pacific Northwest, I worked in a restaurant with a server who was a member of the Umpqua tribe. Every time he got an order for salmon, he would say, "I do not know why white people socially state they support salmon conservancy. They are just going to eat every last one of them out of the river anyway." Only time will tell if he was correct. Personally, I do not eat salmon, but for their sake, I hope he was not right.

The Hume brothers originally started canning salmon in California back in 1864 on the Sacramento River. William, George and John moved to the Columbia River in 1866 to a location called Eagle Cliff in Washington. By 1877, the youngest brother, Robert Hume, was quite prosperous, enabling him to buy the rights to a Rogue River operation that had been a fishery. Hume then built

A label from one of Hume's salmon cans. *Courtesy of Wikipedia.*

a cannery and many other structures and acquired all of the tidelands on the lower part of the river in a move that would impress even J. Astor. This would be the beginning of an industry that would spread to all the waterways in the Pacific Northwest where salmon could be found. Salmon croquettes made from canned salmon became a staple in the dinner lineup in most American households all the way up to the latter part of the twentieth century. This menu item was particularly popular in parts of the country where fresh salmon could not be found. The popularity of canned salmon grew to the point that thirty million pounds of salmon a year were being harvested. It does not take much imagination to realize harvesting at those levels of production would quickly lead to the depletion, demise and devastation of all salmon habitats in the region. Eventually, the canneries abandoned the Rogue and Columbia Rivers, relocating to Alaska.

Restaurants, Breweries and Saloons

Prepared foods offered at hotels and saloons in locations that catered to people headed west or returning from the Plains was very different from the offerings in East Coast cities. In the mid-nineteenth century, American eateries would have continued to offer on their board of fare a style of food that would probably have offended the European palate of world travelers. Reportedly, it would more have been suited for someone who was returning from the western Plains. It seems a sampling of the menu in what we now call the Midwest would have included all kinds of critters that today's patrons would gasp and scream about. Common items would have been quail, squirrel, bear, raccoon, wild boar and turkey. Most may not know it, but in parts of the South, they still eat all of those animals. Probably not so much bear anymore (because they already ate all of them), but as late as the 1960s, I know that in the Ozark mountains, bear was still being eaten, and fried squirrels were generally applauded by most as was stewed raccoon. Stewing was a popular method of preparing that varmint. It takes a lot of rendering to get all the fat off a raccoon. I prefer smoking them before adding the vegetables to this recipe. You can exchange many different protein sources with this recipe. Feel free to use it with any errant neighbor's pet or road kill, too.

You will need:

*A smoker: defined as anything you can light a fire under and put a cover over while controlling a low flame.

*A fire pit with hardwood burned to coals and plenty of smoke rising—even better if there is a metal spit to turn.

*A four-pound raccoon, checked for rabies, cleaned, skinned and splayed.

*Salt and pepper generously and add fresh (or dried) herbs if you have it. Rub into flesh. Place on rack or spit and smoke for as long as you can wait (the longer the better).

If you can, wait until something better comes along. If that happens, you probably will not need this recipe. Just in case, here is the rest of it. An hour before your meat is done start the stew:

Take a couple of onions, a carrot or two, some celery, a couple cans of tomatoes (we are not in the 1850s right now), all chopped to soup size (small enough to fit in a spoon). Sweat everything except tomatoes in a soup pot on medium heat with a little oil or butter. Add tomatoes, salt and pepper to taste. If you have turnips, potatoes or corn, any or all will be great additions, as would bay leaf, paprika, chili powder, cumin, fresh ginger or whatever condiments you prefer. Soy sauce, salsa, ketchup and mustard packs will also work. Add two quarts of water. Bring to a simmer and cook to a stew consistency. Add smoked, deboned raccoon or your varmint de jour. Serve in hot bowls with cornbread and a wilted poke salad (salett) as a side dish—oh yeah, and plenty of hot sauce, too. To drink, I recommend an inexpensive Syrah. Among my acquaintances, I do not think I know of anyone who has ever eaten a raccoon unless they had to. Not that there is anything wrong with it. Now, if you have to, at least you have a recipe.

While restaurants were in their infancy in the Pacific Northwest, the concept of eating away from the home was gaining ground. Louis Eppinger's restaurant at the corner of First Street and A Street in downtown Portland was touted as the place to dine by the *Oregonian*'s social columnist. Eppinger's even offered private rooms for ladies—a very modern idea at the time. Eppinger served a Sunday dinner to impress even the most fashionable palate:

Soup
Chicken Consommé
Fish
Baked Salmon à la Chambord
Cold Dishes
Boned Turkey with Truffles, Ham with Jelly, Smoked Tongue, Chicken Salade
Entrées
Poulet Saute Marengo, Voul al vent Financier, Filet of Veal a la Perigord, Tame Goose with Olives
Vegetables
Asparagus, Cauliflower, Green Peas, New Potatoes, Artichokes
Roasts
Beef, Veal, Spring Lamb with Sauce, Spring Chicken stuffed with Truffles
Dessert
Coffee, Ice Cream, Cabinet Pudding with Wine sauce, Apricots, Cherries, Oranges, Assorted Nuts, Raisins, Assorted Cakes, French Coffee

A menu of that magnitude was quite extensive for Portland in 1883. Impressive was the inclusion of ice cream. I wonder if the dishes were accurate replicas of the French cuisine they were announcing or a hack job similar to the Las Vegas buffets or cruise ship versions of fine-dining cuisine served in those venues today. Eppinger's chef was Victor Laline, a Frenchman from San Francisco who had worked for Eppinger down there too. Eppinger himself had quite the legacy of hospitality accomplishments. After successfully owning and operating a San Francisco saloon, he opened one of the first saloons in Portland in 1877 and his Portland restaurant in 1883. Had he been around today, he would have had the same notoriety as any famous celebrity restaurateurs or chefs.

The godfather of cocktails William Boothby states in his cocktail bible, *World Drinks And How To Mix Them*, that the bamboo cocktail was invented by Eppinger at the Grand Hotel in Yokohama, Japan, in 1899. It is not as popular today as it once was, but it is worth a try for a taste of something different. You can also swap other ingredients for the sherry or vermouth, like a good quality white port from the Douro. Herb-infused liqueurs can stand in for vermouth. It's a fun recipe to play with ingredients.

Bamboo Cocktail

1 shot dry sherry
1 shot dry vermouth
2 dashes orange bitters
2 dashes angostura bitters

Stir and strain then serve with a lemon twist and an olive

Most home cooks in the Pacific Northwest could not have produced a menu like Eppinger's in the latter part of the nineteenth century even if they knew how. Obtaining the products to produce culinary creations of refinement required residing in an area where provisions were readily available. How close you lived to where a steamship docked had everything to do with what you served. That or you and/or your neighbors grew it or raised it. That all changed once the railroads connected the nation, and goods were easily and quickly transported. This also meant that goods could travel both ways, a blessing for all those inland oyster and salmon fans. In 1883, the Occidental Saloon in Tombstone, Arizona, owned by famous Wild West gunslingers Doc Holliday and Wyatt Earp served fresh Columbia River Salmon on the menu of their famous eight-course Sunday repast.

Oysters have been eaten in the Pacific Northwest since the time of its first human inhabitants. A question that has always perplexed me is where and how the consumption of mollusks starts. Archaeological evidence may suggest oysters were consumed from the dawn of humanity forward, but no one knows who first picked one up from the beach and thought, "I think I can eat that." Oysters have been cultivated as far back as the fourth century and were so popular on the East Coast of the United States they had almost depleted them by 1880. Here in the Pacific Northwest, they were just as popular despite the fact that the Lewis and Clark journals reported never seeing any. Somehow, the popularity of this mollusk picked up steam, and restaurateurs capitalized on the ready availability and low cost to procure.

Roscoe Dixon of Astoria was a forward-thinking man when he opened his Astoria eatery on Chenamus Street named Roscoe's First Class Oyster Saloon and invited both ladies and gents—something of a rarity in the 1880s. He did not, however, offer any beverages stronger than coffee or tea. You could go over to Martin Foard and J.J. Stokes of Astoria, located next to the railway, to select a libation. They advertised a full selection of liquors and domestic and imported wines. Loeb and Company, also in Astoria on Main Street opposite of the Parker House, offered a full line of liquors, wines and cigars. The Germania Beer Hall, operating at the same location, whose proprietor was Mr. W.M. Bock, was proudly serving iced draught Weinhard's lager beer out of the wood barrel for a nickel a glass.

In Portland, there were too many breweries in competition in the late 1800s. Henry Weinhard's, Rainier, Kopp's, Lemp's, Mason's, Molson and Oregon Steam are but a few. The competition was fierce; Molson and Sons were fighting the terrible rumor that their beer was being made by "Chinamen." I am not really sure why that would matter or why it would be found egregious enough that the Molson's would attempt to start a PR campaign to battle the dreaded foreign stigma. Even Catholic bishops publically denounced Asians in the newspapers and took some heat in the press for it around the same time.

Taking advantage of the gambling, prostitution and opium seemed to be very popular with the men who made their way through the Pacific Northwest. Beyond comprehension to me is how one might copulate with, buy drugs from and gamble with people that you would not trust to make your beer. Molson had a pretty good recipe, which is probably why the competition used racism, a popular marketing tool in those days to influence locals, and eventually drove the Molson's north. Beer has always been the lubricant of Oregon. No matter how large the wine industry gets here, beer will be the beverage hoisted the most often. The water, hops and grains are the best in the world; probably a testament to that fact is Pacific North westerners (specifically Portlanders) consume more locally made beer than any other locale in the United States.

Bartending in the early days of the Portland waterfront was a lucrative career. Frank Huber was a man of German descent who owned the White House Saloon and the Bureau Saloon—two of Portland's earliest, largest and best saloons. Huber was precise in his service and committed to the principals of true hospitality. Those principals eventually made him a downtown fixture where businesspersons could count on a tasty lunch and a well-made cocktail while conducting their affairs. Louis Eppinger of San

Francisco was the original owner and bartender of the Bureau, which opened in 1877. Eppinger took a partner, W.L. Lightner, in 1879 but sold his interest in 1884. It was at that time Lightner hired Huber as a bartender. Eventually, Lightner sold it to Huber in 1896, when it was renamed Huber's. Frank operated in that location until 1911, when it was moved to 320 Southwest Stark Street, where it still operates.

Other notable Pacific Northwest restaurants operating before the turn of the century were Dunne's English (for steaks and chops) and Zinsley's (for coffee and chocolate). To the north, Holcomb's in Port Townsend did a pretty brisk business, and if you lived around Puget Sound and had a hankering for a clambake, you would head to Butler's Cove just north of Olympia. It was a picnic campground that was very popular for clamming and a new American pastime called recreation. As the turn of the century approached, the Pacific Northwest was luring chefs and entrepreneurs just as it does today and pretty much for the same reasons: inexpensive living costs and opportunities to perfect your craft whether it's brewing, cuisine, distilling, fermenting or viticulture. People here have always been and still are open to trying better food and drink.

THE INVASION OF VITICULTURISTS

Over in Yakima Valley, wine was getting a serious foothold around 1869 with a French winemaker from Alsace named Charles Schanno leading the way, with cuttings procured from the famous Hudson's Bay Company trading outpost at nearby Fort Vancouver. Schanno is also credited with starting the Dalles first brewery in 1867, called Columbia Brewery. In the early days of Pacific Northwest viticulture, three sources provided the cuttings from vines that led to grape production and winemaking. First was the HBC's at Fort Vancouver, second was Henderson Luelling's nursery in Willamette Valley and third was from the first California invasion of would-be winemakers who headed north after the California gold rush did not work out for them.

Grape growing in the Schanno family obviously continued for a generation because in an article from the *Oregonian* on October 10, 1898, listed Emil Schanno from the Dalles displaying his award-winning grapes alongside grapes and wines with A. (Ernest) Reuter (aka Rueter) from Forest Grove at an exposition in Portland. Reuter brought thirty-six bottles of wine made from five varieties of grapes. The columnist for the *Oregonian* brought to light two important issues that many years later some would declare they were the first to realize. Regardless of public opinion, Oregon was not too cool to grow grapes, and Oregon could grow enough different varieties of grapes that importing from other states would no longer be necessary. Turns out Lett, Sommer and Coury were not as ahead of their time as they might have thought.

At the same exposition there was a presentation extolling the virtues of raising hemp particularly the one true hemp, *Cannabis sativa*. As reported in the same article, our government was spending $40 to $50 million importing foreign hemp. The focus of the exhibit was to convince Oregon farmers to raise hemp on their extremely fertile land. Finding concrete evidence as to when that idea caught on is a little hard, but believe me when I tell you, it certainly did. Oregon still grows the finest hemp in the country. It is possible that Colorado and Washington will overtake that position due to recent legislative events. I said possible, but not likely; there is a big difference.

Word of the American Pacific Coast vineyards beginnings had spread to Europe, and viticulturists were invading by the hundreds. From Havre, France, on July 10, 1878, the SS *Labrador* arrived in Portland carrying 438 immigrants. Among them were 200 Swiss immigrants headed to California to cultivate grapes. As they traveled south, I wonder how many found the Willamette, Applegate, Umpqua and Rouge Valleys adequate and put down roots here.

While commercial winemaking in Washington may have gotten its start in Walla Walla, that was all about to change. In 1883, Walla Walla suffered one of the harshest winters on record devastating the vines. This was the same year the intercontinental railroad bypassed Walla Walla, adding to its isolation and halting any farther progress of commercial winemaking until Prohibition had come and gone.

To the south in Canyon City, they did not get a general store until 1862, when Luce & Cozart opened in a tent. By 1880, F.C. Fels was advertising in the *Grant County News* that he could fill all requests of five gallons or less of liquor, beer and wine at his city brewery and saloon. Every newspaper across the territory displayed merchants advertising cold, fresh beer, imported and locally distilled liquors and California or French wines. Local wines were made and sold among the Pacific Northwest enophiles without any formal distribution system. There were at least a dozen vineyards operating in the Chehalem Mountains. Cork-and-bottle advertisements in local newspapers substantiate the fact that a lot of something was being bottled and corked. An advertisement posted in the *Oregonian* from December 23, 1889, verifies Oregon wine was available to the general public. This tidbit contradicts many previous claims from various sources that there were no pre-prohibition Northwest commercial wineries operating. Under the header "Brief Mention," the ad reads, "To enjoy a good Christmas dinner order yourself one dozen bottles of Simon's best Oregon Wine at $4.50 a dozen at 255 Morrison on the corner of 11th."

As was the custom, there were two other mentions in the ad—one for real estate in Astoria and another for pianos. An odd mix of products, but if the typesetter had some space, it seems they would fill it randomly. The most curious piece of this advertisement is the price listed. California bulk wine was eighty cents a gallon, but Charles Wetmore in Lodi was selling his locally produced Sauternes-style wine for six dollars a case. He was growing it from cuttings he brought from Chateau d'Yquem in Bordeaux, and it was even more expensive than his best red wine. Good imported wines at the time were fetching about $2.50 a case. Wine from high-quality Oregon grapes commanded top dollar in 1889, just as they do now. Reuter was building a reputation out in Forest Grove by selling most of his wine in barrels. So much of the commerce in Pacific Northwest wine was done without any government oversight or, most importantly, any taxation. While this was taking place prior to Prohibition, it was kept quiet, and no real records exist to quantify the actual extent of the Willamette Valley wine production in those days. Anyone with a palate for real wine was probably familiar with how much counterfeiting there was of French and other imported wines, and at least if you bought local, you knew what you were getting. Bordeaux started bottling clarets in the current bottle style around 1815, and as early as 1829, there was an American producer, New England Glass, manufacturing the same bottle in volume. They did the same with Champagne-style bottles, too—more evidence counterfeiting not only existed but also flourished. New England Glass even made a statement saying their glass bottles might possibly be found with Bordeaux label vintages dating back prior to 1829.

In addition to the proliferation of domestic products substituted for brand-name imports as well as counterfeits of fine Kentucky bourbons and Tennessee whiskies, there was a newfangled device making its way through the Pacific Northwest that claimed to age wines and liquors with only an electric charge. An article appeared in several newspapers around the Pacific Northwest claiming young wines and whiskies could be aged with electricity. Supposedly, this could be accomplished with just an ordinary electric brush machine with a positive and negative lead. It then required that the operator wrap two carbon blocks with flannel, connect the positive lead to one block and the negative to another and then place them in a container with the wine or whiskey. Then, you would run a charge through it for forty-eight hours for whiskey or two hours for wine. The libation would then be electrically pure and aged, or so the purveyor would like you to believe. The lack of that application's presence in the wine industry today speaks to the fact it was a scam. Well, there is that, and the fact that nobody in a bar ever says, "Hey, bartender, give that a shock, will you please?"

In an article titled "Grapes" printed in the *Willamette Farmer* from Salem, Oregon, on October 17, 1872, the author discusses at length his opinion about some samples of grapes, both foreign and domestic, grown by John Millard of Albany, Oregon. He begins the column by saying, "with these fine specimens before us we conclude grapes can be grown in Oregon." Naming each variety and then expounding on its usage and background, the article leaves the reader with the impression there would be no doubt that vineyards in Oregon could flourish. The grapes sent in to be assessed were Concord, Iona, Isabella, Diana, Adirondack, Rebecca and Delaware for the native selections. The foreign Vitis vinifera varieties were Chasselas Marque, Millers Burgundy (Pinot Meunier), red and white Riesling, Black St. Peters (Zinfandel), Wilder and Warden.

Our grapes were being made into wine. Restaurants were opening so people who wanted to have meals outside the home could dine. Transportation advances have made it possible for the rest of the world to taste Pacific Northwest fruit, seafood, beer and wine. So why does it take another century before the region is recognized as a world-class destination for food and wine? For one thing, what was happening in the Pacific Northwest took a back seat to other issues both domestic and international. Our country was a little preoccupied with flexing its muscles between 1890 and 1920. During that thirty-year period, there were fifty-three U.S. military interventions, nine of them domestic. What people ate and drank in our part of the country was of little importance to anyone other than our fine citizens.

Chapter Ten

Too Much of a Good Thing Means No More Free Lunch

At the end of the nineteenth century, the Pacific Northwest and particularly Portland, Astoria and the Willamette Valley were building reputations—some good, some bad. Willamette Valley's reputation was one of wondrous resources where the finest fertile soil could produce the best fruits, grains, nuts and livestock in America. However, the port cities were developing a different reputation that impugned all who resided there. Portland city commissioners tolerated the gambling, hard drinking and prostitution. They even had a special police division that earned its salary from fees collected for the "Special Police" services. These services were to protect specific business, and the officers assigned to these locations turned a blind eye to activities the regular police would have normally pursued criminal prosecution over. The ménage à trois between special police, crimps and ship captains was the type of enterprise anyone with a larcenous spirit dreams of entering into. Selling able-bodied men into the servitude of ocean-going sea captains, otherwise known as crimping, was a popular vocation at most West Coast cities, including San Francisco. Portland was known as the most dangerous port in the world. During this period, Portland garnered a well-earned reputation as a place where bad things could happen. The crimping (aka shanghaiing) activity was prevalent on the Pacific Northwest Coast during this period because there was a need. Whether the crew jumped ship to mine gold or just went off to build railroads, the ship was unable to sail. When a captain lost his crew, he could not leave until he obtained enough men to sail it. Those circumstances produced a key economic factor for business—supply and demand. Where there is a demand, entrepreneurial entities most often will create a supply. After all, it is the American way. Portland had a reputation for being the most dangerous port in the world from 1890 to 1910. It became one of those legendary stories told among those who knew what the phrase "I've been on the road" actually meant. I was privy to being told the tale one evening about a decade before I knew what being on the road really meant (traveling without any financial means). Hitchhiking, riding the rails and becoming a stowaway all qualify, and if you have done any of those for more than a week, other similar travelers will know. I started traveling early and never stopped. Fortunately, my travels no longer qualify as being on the road in the sense I described previously.

In 1961, I heard about crimping and how dangerous the Pacific Northwest could be from the men who rode the rails of the Missouri Pacific railway where it crossed the Arkansas River from Van Buren to Fort Smith. High up on a bluff, these travelers had a camp I stumbled on. It was in this auspicious location I heard the tale of my first Pacific Northwest story. A warning to be taken seriously by anyone who planned to continue travels as a free man. This warning was explicit and surprising. It went something like this: if you wound up in Portland or Astoria, Oregon, either by land or sea, and had no accompanying mates to keep you safe you could easily become the crew of a ship headed to points west, meaning any port in the Far East, including the famed port of Shanghai. Mind you, this tale was planted firmly in the minds of men who traveled the rails from the time of the railroad's earliest inception, through the Great Depression years and into the decades that followed.

No matter how much warning you might give folks, it might not be enough. The patrons who frequented gambling houses, opium dens and houses of prostitution would be obvious prey because of their status with local law enforcement as "personas non grata," a phrase that has several interpretations. But here it signifies they (those God-fearing, good people) did not value your contribution to the human race. Why law enforcement would not show some gratitude toward the poor souls they were using and abusing to pad their pockets seems wrong to me, but it was not a sentiment the appointed constabularies shared. Unfortunately, in the eyes of the law at that time, "persona non grata" meant you were screwed.

Those poor souls became perfect prey for a crimp. In the beginning, this business was operating on a need to acquire a body when an order came in, but it eventually progressed to keeping-stock-on-hand (bodies-in-captivity) business. Knockout drops or a thump on the head—acquiring the needed bodies was accomplished in many different ways, some more despicable than the two just mentioned. All concluded with the same results. Nothing good was going to come of it. There were days when being shanghaied would have been an improvement over what happed to an unlucky few.

Beyond the distractions in the city (gambling, drinking, prostitution and opium dens), the new arrivals to the Portland waterfront had to beware of an entire community well versed in maritime legislation working in consort with special police and merchants of vice. There was another way for a crimp to collect from a ship captain, and that was to extend credit to sailors for living expenses (including alcohol and gambling debts) while they were ashore. The ability for them to collect expenses and a "per head" set fee (blood money) from any ship captain whom the crimp was able to negotiate a contract with became a well-practiced form of slavery and extortion. At one point, ship captains were declaring legal immunity by posting in the newspaper a declaration that the ship while docked in Portland would not be responsible for any crew member's debts. Although the practice continued until commercial sailing ships no longer plied the seven seas, the exaggeration of exactly how many men were sold off to ship captains has grown over the years. It was a deplorable action and to marginalize it would be a travesty. The self-destructing decadent relationship between sailors, booze and their actions when they came ashore was about as predictable as a heroin or crack addict with money in his or her pocket. A potent mix of predictable behavior for many resulted in a voyage to hell and, most likely, an early demise, and not necessarily in that order. Not a reputation any place wants to be proud of. Saloons did not necessarily create the crimping trade, nor did sailors. The conditions that facilitated the over indulgence of sailors, farmers, townsfolk or anyone else who wandered into a saloon for a drink was just good old-fashioned marketing. Once inside the saloons, they did a good job of keeping you there. Saloon owners came up with all kinds of ingenious ways to keep you there between the gambling, prostitution and food. Patrons were happy until their money ran out or they had to urinate.

The solution to keep men at the bar was as simple as it was disgusting. Most saloons created a trough that ran right beneath the bar like a small culvert with a grate over it and water running through it angled at a pitch to keep flowing. This allowed men to relieve themselves without ever leaving their drink. You could get a lot more drinking done that way. The "Free Lunch" was another saloon specialty that contributed to the demonizing and eventual demise of alcohol sales. For just the price of a five-cent beer, most bars had a buffet of food that ranged from barely edible to well-made food any cook would be proud of. This kept many husbands away from home and helped fuel the frenzy of the fire-and-brimstone message preached by the temperance supporters. With many men spending so much time drinking, gambling and carousing with the working girls, it is easy to see how the women and children left at home might have become resentful, especially when there was no money for household expenses. Most likely, all the earned income was depleted at saloons. The tendency for violent physical abuse associated with male alcohol abusers in their domestic lives was an excessively common occurrence, especially prior to women earning the vote.

Drinking at saloons near the end of the nineteenth century was so out of hand that it began to deteriorate the moral fortitude for most of the men who frequented them. Most considered consuming alcohol not only proper but also patriotic. Because of this, the temperance movement gained steam early on in Portland, long before the introduction of Prohibition in 1914.

The Oro Fino Saloon owned by James Lappeus, Portland's police chief, represented the upscale saloon and brothel where city founders and men with reputations frequented. They operated with a veiled attempt at genuine entertainment, featuring dancing girls who only sang to generate interest in their behind-closed-doors activities upstairs. It was posh but not too pretentious. On the opposite end of the liquor-dispensing denizens of the riverfront were the down and dirty brothels serving every vice known to man such as Nancy Boggs's (otherwise known as Madame of the Willamette River) floating bordello, where fornication and drinking were two of the most popular pastimes.

As the turn of the century loomed, many of the purveyors of vice saw the writing on the wall, especially after the incident at the Webfoot Saloon— well actually, I should say series of incidents. During the first few weeks of April 1874, the Temperance Union prayed and sang hymns at the Webfoot Saloon after two of their members were ejected from the premises by Walter Moffett, the owner, who, out of character and in an angry outburst, referred to the ladies as whores, refusing them service on those grounds. At the time, it was not actually proper etiquette because whores were allowed to drink at bars. An ensuing battle of wills resulted in a lot of bad behavior on everyone's part until a fellow saloon owner and current Police Chief James Lappeus arrested the women. It had to be done, as a crowd had gathered and things were about to get out of hand. It only got worse after the incarceration was instituted. Many do-gooders came to post bail for the temperance workers, which they wholeheartedly refused. The ladies continued the prayers, preaching and hymn singing in the Portland city jail, much to the dismay of the institution's administrators. All the visitors at the jail were causing a

Prohibition. *Courtesy of Library of Congress, Prints & Photographs Division.*

scene that most city administrators did not favor continuing. After visiting hours were over, Police Chief Lappeus burst into the jail and evicted the temperance movement ladies. Exhibiting a bit of common sense, they exited the premises quite unceremoniously. The temperance movement in Portland fizzled and died shortly after the Webfoot Saloon debacle. Walter Moffett sailed off to the South Pacific seas. Word of the temperance protest march incident in Portland spread to smaller towns and created enough of a stir in many churches that citywide dry-status ballots were starting to attract voters.

Who knows, maybe it is what made Edward Von Pessel sell his vineyard. With Prohibition looming, maybe he saw the end nearing and decided to get out while the getting was good. The *Plaindealer*, Roseburg's newspaper, reported in the fall of 1903 a sale of the property he owned had been made to parties from back east and that Mr. Von Pessel would be moving back to California. It does sound like commercial viticulture was thriving enough to warrant a buyer when one of the earliest vineyards in Oregon went up for sale. After all, there were thirteen more possible harvests before enacting and enforcing Prohibition. That's a lot of grapes that could be made into wine. Down in southern Oregon there were saloons but not the kind they had in Portland. They also had a lot of farmers. Farmers ate and drank at home. They would make their own homemade economical wine. Between the farmers, fermentations and the saloons that would serve counterfeit imported labels filled with local wine, most of the local grapes and wine was consumed without the need for distribution. With canned food like coffee and tuna becoming widely available, surviving on the farm was getting easier, and you did not have to go to town as often. But when you did, there were more and more places to eat while you were in town. In those days, if you were looking for a great meal down there in Roseburg, the place to go would have been the new Belle Collins restaurant. I heard they had the best two-bit meal in the city. Yeah, they had a real good reputation.

Home cooks were making dishes that were more elaborate as well, thanks to modern advances in cookery and the availability of products. On June 18, 1905, the *Sunday Oregonian* printed what it called an elaborate dish, chicken chartreuse, an English recipe specifying a one-year-old fowl (the age ensures a tender bird). I took notice of the particular inclusion of canned mushrooms, which were pretty new at the time. It seemed odd in a place where so many wild fresh ones were available for harvesting. This revised version of the recipe would pair well with complex-flavored white wine with above average acidity.

Chicken Chartreuse

1 young hen
12 ounces wild fresh mushrooms, sliced
1 medium onion, diced
1 cup white wine
2 cups heavy cream, scalded
2 slices cooked bacon (optional)
½ cup green peas (optional)
Salt and pepper to taste

Boil or roast a young hen, and then let cool. Remove skin and debone. Dice large pieces into cubes. In a hot sauté pan over high heat, brown 12 ounces of sliced wild fresh mushrooms. Add diced onion to a hot saucepan and

---

cook until translucent. Add cooked mushrooms and chicken, then deglaze with whatever white wine you will be drinking. Add two cups of scalded heavy cream and reduce until thick. Addition of cooked bacon would not hurt it. Add salt and pepper to taste. Serve it over a bed of cooked rice. Noodles or mashed potatoes work well too. If you really want to get crazy, add a half cup of green peas. Garnish with parsley.

This next recipe was a popular vegetarian dish at the turn of the century and a great way to use up seasonal vegetation. It could accompany any grilled meat, and it would pair well as a first course before the chicken chartreuse.

Walla Walla Onions with Summer Corn Stuffing

4 large Walla Walla onions
3 ears of corn
2 tablespoons heavy cream
1 teaspoon melted butter
½ cup mushroom sauce
Salt, pepper and paprika to taste

Blanch four large Walla Walla onions and scoop out the center. Shave three large cooked ears of fresh corn. Place corn pulp in large mixing bowl with two beaten eggs, and then add 2 tablespoons heavy cream, a teaspoon of melted butter and salt, paprika and pepper to taste. Fill the onions with the corn filling, and then cook until heated through and custard is set. Serve with rich cream mushroom sauce. It's a Pacific Northwest signature dish; too bad this isn't served on any menus today, as someone could build quite a reputation with a dish like this.

Onions make or break many a culinary creation, and when cooks have problems getting onions, it is a big problem. Just such a scenario was the

Pike Place Market, Seattle, Washington, circa 1930s. *Courtesy of Municipal Archive.*

impetus for the birth of one of, if not the most famous, Pacific Northwest landmarks. I am speaking of Pike Place Market. In 1906–07, the price of onions in Seattle skyrocketed with a ten-fold increase in price. Angry citizens blamed the produce middlemen. Their complaints were answered by a Seattle city councilman, Thomas Revelle, who proposed an open-to-the-public street market that would connect products to the buyers, and on August 17, 1907, Pike Place Market in Seattle was born. That morning, eight farmers brought wagons full of produce to First and Pike. Ten thousand eager customers greeted the farmers, and they completely sold out of their products by 11:00 a.m. It was a huge success from the very beginning, and Pike Place Market became the place to go. It was the destination to see and be seen for decades to come, not to mention a great place to shop.

Back down in Oregon there was some serious fermenting going on, and we are not talking sauerkraut. Well, they were doing that too, but that is a different story. In the Chehalem Mountains, there were several grape growers who were quietly building a reputation for world-class wines. That reputation came with a following of wine-thirsty fans who snapped them up without even being bottled—they were buying by the barrel.

The lush and beautiful farmland at the base of the coast range to the west of Portland around Cornelius and Forest Grove was one of those places that was building a great reputation for Oregon not just as a place where the best timber in the country could be grown. The area had a stagecoach line in 1866 that connected it to Portland. In 1869, a sternwheeler that carried passenger and freight arrived, and by 1871, train tracks had been laid. Beyond the advances in transportation, the area was making a name for itself in higher education with Pacific University breaking ground in 1849. Anchored with an accredited university and the start of a horticulture revolution (daffodil bulbs), Forest Grove was building a reputation, including a guy who was making some pretty special wine on Wine Hill. No Oregon wine story is complete without a significant homage to F.W. David and Reuter, a couple of the pioneers who grew red burgundy (Pinot noir) in Forest Grove long before any of those guys in the 1960s who came up from California.

If one were to say there was a birthplace of Pinot noir in Oregon, it would have to be Forest Grove. Well, that is if you believe the report compiled by the 1901 Oregon Agricultural Experiment Station in Corvallis, Oregon, in Bulletin 66, titled, "The Grape in Oregon Part I: Western Oregon" by E.R. Lake. The compilation of this report was to help amateur grape growers obtain accurate information about which grapes to plant and where to plant them. To compile this information, the Oregon Agricultural Experiment Station in Corvallis sought out the wisdom of the few people growing grapes commercially. Out in Forest Grove and the Chehalem Mountain area, the guys who had been at it the longest and were considered to have the most experience at running a commercial vineyard operation were A.F Reuter and F.W. David, for whom David Hill was named. According to Reuter, the "Sweetwater, Zinfandel, Burgundy, Black Hamburg, Muscatel, Red Mountain, Chasselas Fountainbleu, Delaware, and Muscat are excellent for our purposes (winemaking)." August Aufranc down in Salem, known for his proficiency with raising award-winning poultry, was also growing grapes and preferred White Chasselas, Red Burgundy and Concord.

G.W. McReynolds from Lane County cultivated Green Mountain and Diamond with good results. This study from the experimental agricultural station illuminates best soil types and site locations. The article repeatedly refers to where and how the profitable vineyards farm their grapes. They also discourage any home growers from attempting to plant *Vitis vinifera*, stating it could be done in Oregon but should be left to professionals.

In October 1904, an *Oregonian* staff writer who went by the initials A.D. took an artist named Milton Werschkv out to Forest Grove to develop a story about the world-class wines that A.F. Reuter was making on David Hill. The article, "Making Wine in the Chehalem Hills of Oregon" reports on the efforts of this phenomenal winemaker who, for many years, quietly produced excellent wines without drawing attention to himself, and probably for good reason. The fine townsfolk down in Forest Grove were the abstaining-from-alcohol, temperance-supporting and church-going, hey-let's-make-it-a-dry-town type of folks.

In fact, they did make the town dry in 1897, well before the national enactment of Prohibition. In A.D's article, he states that the existence of the wine business in those hills was not common knowledge in Portland. At the time, most city folks were whiskey and beer men. Reuter was fond of entering his wine into contests at expositions and agricultural events. It was the main reason he bottled some of this wine. He took first prize at the 1898 Transcontinental Exposition in Omaha, Nebraska. The judges spoke of his wine in glowing adoration compared to the entries from California and New York. Reuter entered his Rhine/Kelvner-style wine, described as "a wine pure and delicate in quality, with a perfect color and a bouquet unrivaled," pretty eloquent verbiage for a wine from the newcomer way out there in Oregon. In 1904, he entered the St. Louis Exposition, held in honor of the Louisiana Purchase, and won a silver medal. With these accolades, Reuter pioneered the Willamette Valley wine industry, creating a legacy all enophiles should know.

Another article validating the existence of a commercial viticulture business in Oregon appeared in the *Morning Oregonian*. In 1908, Walter Hoge wrote an article called "Viticulture in the Willamette Valley." He extolled the expertise of Forest Grove grape growers who had been achieving quality harvests since 1878, again citing F.W. David as the first and Reuter as the second. Wines from Fredrick David's wine hill won first prize at exhibitions in Chicago and Buffalo, New York. Hoge spoke about site selection as if it was old news. Seems they all were keen to southern-facing hill slopes, even way back then. Some of the growers included William Koppel, J. A. Peterson, A. Anderson, F. Bile, R. Holischer and several others who were producing grapes at successful vineyards.

The proof that cold-climate grapes from Europe could grow in Oregon was pretty much common knowledge by the 1880s, and the *Morning Oregonian* printed an article called "All Fruit of North Temperate Zone Reach Perfection in Oregon." Mr. Wilbur K. Newell, the president of the state horticulturist

The Quileute tribe has a small fleet of fishing vessels that regularly engage in the marine fishery. The two important commercial marine stocks are Dungeness crab and groundfish. *Courtesy of Pamela Heiligenthal.*

A totem pole in front of River's Edge Restaurant in La Push, Washington, reflects the area's Native American influence on the Quileute Indian Reservation. *Courtesy of Pamela Heiligenthal.*

A-Ka-Lat or James Island, thousands of winters before the arrival of the White Drifting–House people (ho-kwats), the Quileute Indians and the ghosts of their ancestors lived and hunted on this island. *Courtesy of Pamela Heiligenthal.*

Inception of Birth of Oregon, Theodore Gegoux, 1923. *Courtesy of Oregon State Parks and Recreation Department: State Archives Holdings.*

Hillcrest Vineyard, 2013. *Courtesy of Pamela Heiligenthal.*

Luisa and Maria Ponzi. *Courtesy of Ponzi Vineyards.*

David Hill Winery and Vineyard. *Courtesy of David Hill Winery and Vineyard.*

Modernist Cuisine authors, *from left to right*: Maxime Bilet, Chris Young and Nathan Myhrvold. *Photo courtesy of Ryan Matthew Smith, Modernist Cuisine, LLC.*

The Cooking Lab, located in Bellevue, Washington, is the culinary research laboratory and publishing company originally created for Modernist Cuisine. *Courtesy of Ryan Matthew Smith, Modernist Cuisine, LLC.*

Modernist Cuisine sous-vide steak. *Courtesy of Melissa Lehuta, Modernist Cuisine, LLC.*

Modernist Cuisine tilapia. *Courtesy of Melissa Lehuta, Modernist Cuisine, LLC.*

Red wine spill. *Courtesy of Ryan Matthew Smith, Modernist Cuisine, LLC.*

David Hill Winery & Vineyard. *Courtesy of Douglas Remington, Ethereal Light Photography, LLC.*

King Estate Winery, Eugene, Oregon. *Courtesy of Pamela Heiligenthal.*

A view from the guesthouse at King Estate Winery, Eugene, Oregon. *Courtesy of Pamela Heiligenthal.*

Grilled oysters with chermoula on a bed of rock salt. Paley's Place Bistro & Bar, 2013. *Courtesy of Pamela Heiligenthal.*

Marc Hinton's special crab cakes. *Courtesy of Pamela Heiligenthal.*

Maine Day Boat Lobster: Avocado, pole beans, tarragon, sweet pea sprouts, chervil and extra virgin olive oil. Noisette Restaurant, Portland, Oregon. *Courtesy of Pamela Heiligenthal.*

Moulard Duck Breast: Kale & fingerling puree with veal sweetbread, savory cabbage, kamut and ramano bean ragout with port wine sauce. Noisette restaurant, Portland, Oregon. *Courtesy of Pamela Heiligenthal.*

Fresh free-range eggs from the Dancing Chicken Farm, La Center, Washington. *Courtesy of Pamela Heiligenthal.*

Organically grown berries from the Pacific Northwest. *Courtesy of Pamela Heiligenthal.*

Organically grown berries from the Pacific Northwest. *Courtesy of Pamela Heiligenthal.*

Organically grown West Coast heirloom tomatoes. *Courtesy of Pamela Heiligenthal.*

Organically grown vegetables from the Pacific Northwest. Portland Farmer's Market, Portland State University. *Courtesy of Pamela Heiligenthal.*

Organically grown lobster mushrooms from the Pacific Northwest. Portland Farmer's Market, Portland State University. *Courtesy of Pamela Heiligenthal.*

Adam Campbell, Elk Cove, 2012. *Courtesy of Pamela Heiligenthal.*

Red wine of the Pacific Northwest. *Courtesy of Pamela Heiligenthal.*

Halibut with artichoke and air-dried heirloom tomato. Canlis Restaurant, Seattle, Washington. *Courtesy of of Canlis restaurant.*

Below: Beets and pears paired with blue cheese and bitter greens. Canlis Restaurant, Seattle, Washington. *Courtesy of Canlis restaurant.*

Organically grown rainier cherries from the Pacific Northwest. *Courtesy of Pamela Heiligenthal.*

Dundee, Oregon vineyard view. *Courtesy of Douglas Remington, Ethereal Light Photography, LLC.*

board, championed the efforts of a lot of local wine-grape growers that had made a reputation for flawless fruit. He went on to state that Jackson and Josephine Counties were well suited for *Vitis vinifera*, particularly Muscat, Tokay and Malagra grapes. Men such as Peter Britt of Jacksonville, A.H. Carson of Grants Pass, A.R. Shipley of Oswego and John F. Broetje of Milwaukee were all noted viticulturists, and Newell lauded them for their efforts and success in an article written in 1908, just ahead of Prohibition.

Jacob Doerner, one of the earliest Oregon grape cultivators, was defending his vineyard from bears in the Roseburg area in 1913. Probably not the actions of a man who thought wine production would cease in a couple of years. The fact that the newspaper reported the bear attack signified grape cultivation had risen to a level at which a man might risk his life to continue the enterprise or that the wine he made was good enough to fight a bear over. A hungry bear can eat a lot of grapes in a short period of time, and once they are gone, it's not like they will grow back in a couple of weeks. Most vineyard owners today, if faced with the same problem, would probably take the same action, resulting most likely with a lot of bear meat eaten by the family of that vineyard owner—well, that is if people still ate bear meat. I'm sure they do on rare occasions where and when hunting bear is allowed, or you have to put one down in your garage or backyard. In 1947, Meta Given in her *Modern Encyclopedia of Cooking* included a good tutorial on preparing bear. Pretty good evidence bear consumption in the twentieth century was probably more common than we may have thought.

Teetotalers and the temperance movement were gaining popularity around the same time grapevines all over the Pacific Northwest were starting to reach maturity. Unfortunately for the winemakers, it was also the same time the women of Washington and Oregon gained the right to vote. Just as the wine industry here was blossoming, Prohibition loomed ever closer. For the early wine industry, it was a real shame. Too much work went into those vines to keep them alive, producing juice for upwards of thirty years. It was a shame that they were pulled up like weeds.

Pre-Prohibition statutes allowed for the legal production of two hundred gallons of homemade wine without paying taxes. Somehow, many people went through the entire time span of Prohibition believing the law included homemade wine. It was allowed—but it was not legal. Much like marijuana today, in some states under certain circumstances, it is allowed—but it is not legal.

Beer was a different story. Just as the temperance movement was gaining ground, William Painter in Baltimore invented the crown cap.

Beer bust and barn raising at the Burrowes farm. *Courtesy of Museum & Arts Center of the Sequim-Dungeness Valley, Washington.*

It's the same technology still used today to seal beer bottles. Besides the best water and hops in the world, there were two components that made the brewers successful in the Pacific Northwest—the bottle cap and the railroads. Sealing a beer bottle so it could travel changed everything for that industry. Railroads created a way to move massive amounts of freight inland, affording saloons all along the rails distribution from Northwest brewers. The Pacific Northwest beer industry began to expand like its sibling wine industry, and it, too, was demolished by national prohibition.

For many in the Pacific Northwest, the turn of the century was a sweeping moment in time. Progress and commerce were moving quickly due to transportation advances, and the gold strikes up and down the west coast put a lot of cash in people's pockets while bolstering the local economy. The national temperance fever that was sweeping the nation was like a tidal wave. In Oregon and Washington, women achieved the right to vote before the state mandated Prohibition. The women of the Pacific Northwest heavily influenced the outcome of temperance ballot measures across the region. On a national level, women gaining the vote here had to fuel the fire for the suffragette movement across the country, ultimately resulting in the ratification of the Nineteenth Amendment.

Five years prior to the enactment of national Prohibition and the first year women had the right to vote, the voters of Washington and Oregon passed an amendment to the state constitutions on November 3, 1914. Those amendments prohibited the manufacture, sale or advertisement of intoxicating liquor in both states and were to take effect on January 1, 1916.

With only a couple of years to get ready before the taps were shut off, there were many changes taking place. All of the businesses owners that were willing to cross the line from legitimate, law-abiding citizens to illegitimate restaurant operations had their work cut out for them. If Google had been around back then, a search query of "How do I turn a saloon into a restaurant" would have been trending in 1914. In a way, Prohibition probably helped the alcohol business. Selling illicit wine, beer and distilled liquors created a completely new economy. It also brought together people from diverse backgrounds that would have never done business or socialized together. Just ask anyone who has ever sold illicit drugs. All you have to do is to forbid it and they will all want it.

Nobody knows how much Pacific Northwest wine was sold in Canada. Plenty of liquor from Ireland and Scotland made its way down from Canada. I doubt the boats went back empty. Smuggling is a vocation, and only the truly talented survive at it. I am sure many rum runners made sure they did it proficiently. Loosely translated, a load of goods down means a load of something should go back for maximum profitability. Oregon and Washington wine that could be represented as Mosel, Rhine, Burgundy Bordeaux or Kelvner wine would sell well in Canadian cities labeled authentically as French, German or Austrian wines.

In a letter to the editor of the *Oregonian* on the first day of Prohibition, Jean Wilbur muses on changes Prohibition will bring to the Third Street area of downtown Portland. She proffers a list of all the great merchants and commercial opportunities in the area and says that most of the saloons were already making plans to become restaurants (most likely speakeasies) offering amusement and light refreshments. The gist of her rambling was to point out how the new legislation was not affecting merchants or commerce and everything would be just fine.

There are a couple of things Prohibition brought about that do not usually get any consideration when that era is looked back on. First, banning of the sale of alcohol presented the perfect opportunity for anyone with stock on hand to completely deplete his inventory, regardless of quality. I am sure many producers nowadays would kill for that situation to present itself again. Second, for some winemakers and real distillers (not moonshiners), it gave those producers time to properly age their products if they had deep enough pockets while they waited it out. After all, private ownership and consumption of alcohol was not illegal. Regardless of what your alcohol intake was prior to Prohibition, the increase in binge drinking spiked due to the mass hysteria created by shutting-down sales. Too many people were drinking like each drop of alcoholic libation might be their last, and that was not a good thing. Attitudes like that only fueled the fervor and validity of the message the Temperance Union was trying to convey. We all know how this thing turns out, but amid all the newfangled technology that blossomed in this era, it will be interesting to see how this mess gets untangled.

Chapter Eleven

Telephones, Cars and Radios

Prohibition Halts Progress

January 1, 1916, ended the legitimate sale of alcoholic beverages in Washington and Oregon. National Prohibition, the Eighteenth Amendment and the Volstead Act, would not happen until 1919. With saloons no longer operating, and consequently no more free lunches offered to keep their patrons at the bar, serving prepared foods for profit started to gain ground. On that subject, many have written about the devastation of the restaurant industry after Prohibition. Without the profit liquor brought, no one could stay profitable enough to be open. The truth is, only the poorly managed restaurants went out of business because of Prohibition. Well-run restaurants with good food all of a sudden had a new customer base. Most working men prior to Prohibition took advantage of the saloon's free lunch. Without those places, the lunch crowd had to find new eateries. The fact that patrons only paid for the drinks previously meant that close scrutiny of the food probably did not happen. A sober man paying for food had much higher expectations, so only restaurants with food worth paying for survived.

Even today, with all the food-serving establishments that serve at least beer and wine, there are restaurants that do not serve alcohol and do well. On the other side of the coin, then, there were the speakeasies operating as entertainment venues or restaurants that disguised their drinks, and they certainly prospered during Prohibition. Almost 50 percent of Portland's former saloons were refitted as poolrooms, restaurants and soda fountains during Prohibition. The sudden popularity of soda stands created an opportunity, and many decided to convert their businesses to clandestine liquor outlets. For them, it was an easy juncture. After all, it was their business to make drinks. One of the more notorious moral squad arrests happened in Portland during a railroad strike. Police took notice that the striker's headquarters was Billy Smith's Soft Drink Emporium on Russell Street. Railroad men were not the soft drink–sipping kind. It looked like the kind of place that needed looking into and arrests followed soon thereafter.

Speaking of arrests, on January 2, 1918, Internal Revenue Agents found seventeen barrels containing more than eight hundred gallons of wine, which they confiscated, in a Vancouver home on Burnt Bridge Road, as reported by the *Morning Oregonian*. Curiously, the article mentions the ethnicity of the men arrested and so began the demonizing of Italian Catholics for their alcohol-loving ways. I guess someone had to blame something for making people drink. Anytime you have to produce large quantities of anything and deliver it to your customers, it takes some organization; otherwise, it won't get done. Catch a few Italians with some wine, and all of a sudden, it is organized crime, and a whole nationality becomes the victim of profiling.

Looking over all the arrests reported in the newspapers during this period, you can find that there were two common denominators. Law enforcement always found wine, and the arrestee was usually an Italian. Another anomaly I find curious is that the wine that showed up in these raids was usually in barrels or carboys, signifying it was local wine—another indicator commercial winemaking did exist in Oregon before the end of Prohibition.

In Oregon and Washington, drugstores could sell alcohol for medicinal purposes during Prohibition. Between January and March 1916, more than fifty new drug stores opened in Seattle. Washingtonians most often procured their alcohol at the local drugstore, and two years into Prohibition, new legislation started to close that loophole. Detective P.D. McKay, a Tacoma, Washington police inspector, went on record stating that in the past, it was not uncommon for three to five hundred quarts of spirits to be sold a day in drugstores around Tacoma under the guise of medicinal use. Detective McKay went on to say that through enforcement of new city regulations, the sale had dropped to only fifty quarts a day. On average, Oregon drugstores saw a 1,000 percent increase in alcohol sales in the first year of Prohibition.

I'm sure all the physicians appreciated the boon in business from patients requesting a prescription for alcohol. Doctors wrote so many prescriptions that we had to import alcohol from out of the country to fill them. Destroying all the liquor when Prohibition was enacted was a bit premature. Had people come to their senses and found a moral backbone? Not likely. Sounds more like bootleggers had successfully taken a larger share of the market with adequate product quality, competitive prices and a steady supply.

A new vocation and industry appeared soon after Prohibition enactment, and that was the fabrication of distilling equipment. On June 6, 1921, the Portland Police Department's morals squad raided the home of E.V. Mariman at 953 East Twenty-sixth Street. It took two trucks to haul away all the wine and equipment to make stills. Judge Rossman, who for some reason seemed to catch all the cases that involved alcohol, tried the case. Could there be anything worse than a temperance-promoting judge with political aspirations back then? Not if you were on the wet side of the wet/dry debacle. For some who held public office, the new morality that Prohibition ushered in was like giving a pastor the power to hand out fines if you did not come to church. On the flip side were the corrupt policemen who used the system to line their pockets.

Many factors contributed to the changing tide regarding the wet/dry battle. Although Oregon and Washington had already enacted statewide prohibition when World War I broke out, the national Prohibition was influenced by that conflict. On many levels, carrying out the work that needed to be done to make Prohibition effective was something the folks who wanted it to take place had no idea how to get done. The temperance movement was proficient at political maneuvers but not so great at figuring out how to make the legislation operational. When the Eighteenth Amendment was enacted, the legislation was so vague that a commission was convened to define the legislation, resulting in the creation of the Volstead Act to give the law some definition.

The arrival of automobiles, telephones and radios helped people keep their minds off drinking to a certain extent, as there was not much else to keep one entertained and connected before these inventions came about. These conveniences also aided bootleggers and smugglers in avoiding detection by law enforcement while they went about the business of delivering products.

Now, I know most of you were following that train of thought. Cars and telephones, you might say, yeah, they were big technological advancements and certainly played an important role in helping bootleggers and rum runners avoid prosecution, but radio? Radio was a really big deal in the 1920s. It was very new, recently declassified from military-only use. From Schenectady, New York, in October 1920, Union College aired what is believed to be the first public-entertainment broadcast in the United States using the call letters 2ADD. It was probably not too surprising that when authorities realized Seattle's most notorious bootlegger owned the first radio station in Seattle, they raised a few eyebrows.

Prohibition Dry Squad members in 1919, King County, Seattle. *Courtesy of Seattle Metropolitan Police Museum.*

The title of Pacific Northwest's most notorious bootlegger has to go to Roy Olmstead, a Seattle policeman who started his illicit alcohol career while he was still on the police force. He was not part of the Seattle Dry Squad, a group tasked with raiding homes and businesses suspected of violating the liquor ban during Prohibition, but he was involved in many raids and arrests of bootleggers.

Roy was one of the corrupt policemen who saw the potential for profit in bootlegging early on. Officer Olmstead was known as a "good bootlegger." Olmstead earned this reputation by operating his operation like a well-run business. No guns, no other criminal activities and no diluting of the product were allowed. Olmsted's business grew so large that by 1924, he was one of the largest employers in the King County area. This also happened to be the year that Roy divorced his wife and married Elise Campbell. That same year, Roy partnered up with a young radio engineer named Alfred Hubbard. Olmstead and Hubbard formed the American Radio Telephone Company. Hubbard proceeded to build a one-thousand-watt transmitter, and now, the biggest bootlegger in Seattle owned a broadcasting company. The new Mrs. Olmstead became a regular on the radio station, hosting a children's bedtime-story show. Turns out the programming for the children's bedtime-story show was actually coded messages directing Roy's rum running boats operating in Puget Sound. As criminal relationships often do, this one went bad when Hubbard decided to turn state's witness against Olmstead. Curiously, the promise of a badge as an enforcement agent was all the enticement needed to make Hubbard turn on his partner. Roy was fined $8,000, did four years of serious time and came close to having his conviction overturned when the case reached the Supreme Court, where he lost. Oddly enough, when President Roosevelt took office, he gave Olmstead a full pardon and refunded his $8,000 dollars of fines.

One of the good things that helped the future of Northwest wineries was the producers who kept growing grapes for personal winemaking. There was a lot more of that going on than anyone wants to admit, even today. Out in Helvetia, Oregon, a small unincorporated community in Washington County drew its fair share of Swiss and German immigrants. Jakob Yungen planted vines on the opposite side of the hill that led down to the Willamette River, and he was a wine pioneer that held fast to the right to make wine for medicinal purposes. The Swiss Club also enjoyed the fruit of the vines produced from grapes grown on Grape Hill before Prohibition, during Prohibition and for many decades after. Helvetia Winery is still in operation today. Applegate and Umpqua Valleys also provided a lot of fruit for home and sacramental wine use. In Washington, the Upland Winery, planted in 1914 by William P. Bridgman in Sunnyside, Washington, not only survived prohibition but also flourished by the time of repeal. He had 165 acres of *Vitis vinifera* growing. Charles Somers in the western part of the state was cultivating Island Belle at the St. Charles Winery on Stretch Island in Puget Sound.

Up until Prohibition, wine consumption in the Pacific Northwest was generally an at-home-with-dinner activity or relegated to dinner events when dining was usually a bit more formal. Soon, locally grown grapes turned into homemade wine had replaced the prevalence of consuming commercial whiskey at the saloon. In a way, home wine consumption during Prohibition inspired the expansion of locally grown grapes. When the laws were repealed, there was a much larger customer base than there was before, and home wine drinkers were eager for the return of professionally produced wine pretty much for the same reasons home winemaking is not very popular today. Producing high-quality wine at home is not as easy as producing well-brewed beer. Throughout Prohibition, Pacific Northwest beer lovers could get the taste of beer in the many different choices called near beer. Weinhard's and Blitz made their versions. I think this comment about near beer summed up the product pretty well: "Whoever called it near beer was a poor judge of distance!" Near beer had only .5 percent alcohol, and it sold in the beginning. But soon, producers could not give it away. Brewers then started selling malt concentrate that was like instant beer. Add water and yeast and wait a few weeks for fermentation to complete. All the major brewers sold malt extract in grocery stores. Not only were they supplying home-brewers, they supplied the bootleggers too.

A byproduct of Prohibition was Americans' insane love affair with sweets. Sure, we had many sweets on our tables and in our diets before the Eighteenth Amendment, but after the removal of alcohol from diets, most people would crave sugar because the liver needs sugar to repair itself. Sweets cookbooks and new confectionary foods were becoming a national pastime. MoonPies, Chase's Cherry Mash, Hostess Cupcakes, Yoo-hoo, marshmallow fluff, apple crisp, icebox cake, Eskimo Pies, Clark Bars, Gummi Bears, chocolate truffles, Pez, Twizzler, pineapple upside-down cake, Twinkies and s'mores were all invented between 1918 and 1933. I'm sure I missed a few in that list, but you get the picture.

Prior to the existence of television, fairs and expos were popular venues for entertainment, and fair food, just as it is today, was often fried, sweet and excessive in its appeal to gluttony. The following recipe has survived for more than a century:

> ### Pressed Pastry Cooked in Melted Butter
> #### AKA the Funnel Cake, Circa 1879
>
> 200 milliliters water
> 100 grams butter
> 200 grams fine flour
> 5 eggs
> Grated rind of ½ lemon
> 1 tablespoon sugar
> Oil, lard or butter for frying
>
> *Bring water and butter to a boil. Gradually add the flour and stir until the dough turns dry and does not stick to the pot. Remove the pot from the fire. To the hot mixture, add 1 egg, lemon rind and sugar. When cooled, gradually add the remaining eggs, one at a time. The dough is then firmly beaten. Add to a pastry bag or syringe and then eject into the hot melted oil, lard or butter. Cook until golden brown. Flip and remove when both sides are browned. Dust with powdered sugar and cinnamon.*

This dish has evolved to its newest incarnation: the Mexican funnel cake, served with strawberry sauce and whipped cream. This variation started appearing at fairs around 2008. The churro vendors had to come up with something to combat the business they were losing to the funnel cake stands. I'm sure somewhere right now there is a calzone shop owner planning to come up with something the Stromboli guy does not have. Churros or funnel cake fried dough is fried dough, no matter how you garnish it.

Besides the plethora of sweets, there were many other unintended consequences to the Eighteenth Amendment, some with far-reaching social implications. Jazz music just appeared on the scene, getting its foothold in New Orleans around 1910. With that get-up-off-your-ass-and-shake-your-booty beat, the sound appealed to a diverse crowd of fans who saw no race and no gender discrimination. The intermingling of sexes and races followed, angering the conservatives who had ushered in Prohibition. The insolence exhibited by the Bible-thumping, teetotaling, temperance-loving folks who were able to bring to bear the full weight of the Eighteenth Amendment on every sinning soul in America was not surprising. Jazz clubs served illicit alcohol from the get go. Years after Prohibition, they would still sell illicit alcohol, and why not? They were the go to places to get your heroin, cocaine, opium, hashish (if you were lucky) and marijuana. Worrying about a little alcohol was the least of their concerns. The profits from illegal drugs and alcohol also generated support from the organizations who were supplying the product in the way of police protection.

How many women drank behind closed doors pre-Prohibition was grossly underestimated. The arrests of white women found drinking in clubs during Prohibition shocked the Protestants of white-bread America. Women gaining the right to vote did many things, including making a declaration to go and drink where and when they wanted. The vote helped break down many other barriers and preconceived morality boundaries. This subject has not received the attention it deserves. Portland's political establishment told it like it was when, in 1922, they arrested and suspended the operating license of R.D. Stuart. Stuart was an established businessman who owned an African American entertainment establishment. He did not discriminate and was consequently punished.

In those days, when your presence was not appreciated in a community, these guys would leave you some subtle hints—something like leaving a note on your door telling you to get out of town. Setting a cross on fire on your lawn or at your business would occur if you did not leave. The next escalation would be lynching or abduction. The Ku Klux Klan in the 1920s reportedly had 200,000 members in Oregon and almost as many supporters in Washington who supported Prohibition and of course, extreme racism.

Stuart did not refuse white people when they came to his cabaret, although he knew it was not smiled on by the local police to allow white women to dance with black men. A black woman dancing with a white man was not a problem to the police for some reason. Stuart lost his business license for his beliefs in equality, and Portland mayor Baker showed what a jerk he could be with his definition of decency.

Down in Salem, the Klan was very active. Charles Maxwell, a businessman in Salem who started with a shoeshine stand, was harassed by the KKK in 1921. He was told in no uncertain terms that it was time for him to leave. Stalwart and unyielding, Maxwell not only stayed but also opened a restaurant called Fat Boy BBQ, and it survived until the Depression, when a lack of business caused his operation to foreclose. Oregon has a long history of not acting as a state located north of the Mason-Dixon line. The timeline of Oregon's racial laws indicates the extremism of this state's beliefs. Not only did we literally exterminate almost all of the indigenous peoples, but we also attempted to exclude all black people from any civil rights for as long as possible.

The biggest unforeseen consequence of the experiment called Prohibition was the loss of $11 billion in tax revenues and the $300 million it cost to unsuccessfully enforce the laws the government had enacted. Those figures do not include any numbers from the loss of revenue from wineries, breweries and distilleries that were closed down or all the jobs lost by those industries. However, bringing alcohol back was more complicated than most people know, and it did not happen overnight. Repeal came gradually. First President Roosevelt legalized 3.2-percent beer and wine through the Cullen-Harrison Act on March 22, 1933. Then, on December 5, 1933, the ratification of the Twenty-first Amendment repealed the Eighteenth Amendment.

How long did it take the alcoholic-drinks business to gather its respective thoughts and get the ball rolling again? Move on to the next page to find out.

Chapter Twelve

Post-Prohibition and the Unspoken '40s and '50s

C losing the door to the great experiment that was Prohibition was not much of a consolation considering the hardships that came with the Great Depression. With economic conditions crippling the local economy, Northwest citizens were well aware of the revenues alcohol would bring to the municipalities and the many jobs those industries provided in the past. It would take a while for the legitimately distilled spirits and freshly brewed beer to appear, and most people for a while got alcohol from wherever they were already getting it. Washington and Oregon adopted the Twenty-first Amendment at the same time but many states did not. Mississippi did not ratify it until 1966 and there are still ten states with dry counties.

For northern Washingtonians, a trip across the border to Canada would remain a popular distraction. Pacific Northwest restaurants that served drinks through Prohibition had a loyal following that continued. That loyalty was strong enough to sustain quite a few of those restaurants for a while. In fact, some are still operating today—such as Huber's, Portland's oldest restaurant, and Jake's Famous Crawfish. Then, in Bellingham, Washington, there is the Horseshoe Café; in Seattle, the Rendezvous Restaurant and Lounge; and the Spar, the Radonich brothers' place, in Old Town Tacoma, just to name a few. The hardships of the Depression let up a little after the repeal of Prohibition, but just when things were picking up steam, along came World War II, putting a damper on all aspects of the food and beverage industry. But let's get on to talking about the drinking.

Going back as far as the days of the British occupation in the Pacific Northwest, there has always been wine produced from local grapes, whether it was *Vitis vinifera* or *labrusca*. On the Washington side of the Columbia River, plantings exceeded that of the Willamette Valley. Everywhere in the Pacific Northwest, alcohol in all forms was being made and consumed. Fermenting fruit juice into wine was carried out throughout the region, as was the fermentation and distillation of grains, with or without government approval. This took place before the first prohibition in the Oregon Territory back in 1844 and continues to this day.

One thing that did not change post-Prohibition was how different the lives of people living in metropolitan areas were from their rural counterparts. Eating and drinking habits were very different; the evolution of eating outside the home was a slow one for rural areas. When it came to public consumption of alcohol, in most rural areas it was frowned on unless you were Catholic. If you happened to reside in a city or pretty good-sized town, you could grab a drink without everyone knowing about it, or for that matter, anyone even caring about it. A good example regarding drinking and dining progress in metropolitan areas was the opening of a Trader Vic's franchise in Seattle. In 1940, Victor Jules Bergeron Jr. started the themed-restaurant-chain concept when he chose to open a second location in the Pacific Northwest. The first was on San Pablo Avenue in Oakland, California. Although those locations have since closed, the concept still lives on with several restaurants continuing to inebriate guests on a daily basis.

In rural communities, a trip to the grocery store or gas station probably gave you a view of everyone's vehicle parked outside the bar. Come the following Sunday in every Protestant church after the service, the conversation would eventually turn to gossip and who was out drinking—a favorite subject for those who liked to engage in such nonsense. They did not consider discussing who had been drinking as gossip. The evangelical church sanctions such social profiling as plotting a strategy to save poor sinners' souls whether they (the sinners) want to participate or not.

Many people in the Pacific Northwest made wine at home before and during Prohibition, and many of them made more than they could drink. Selling the extra wine to neighbors was an activity practiced by most. On Stretch Island in Puget Sound, where a lot of retiring Seattleites purchased land, many considered growing grapes a lucrative second income during Prohibition. To avert the attention of law enforcement, one only needed access to mature grapes with adequate sugar levels. There were plenty of places in Oregon and Washington to obtain grapes with Brix (sugar) levels between 21 and 24. This assured completion of fermentation without the necessity of purchasing large amounts of sugar that might raise enough eyebrows to merit a visit from a local constabulary. Fortunately for Pacific Northwest residents, most pre-Prohibition grape growers continued to cultivate their vineyards after the enactment of the Eighteenth Amendment.

The scale of wine production in the Pacific Northwest was miniscule compared to what it is today, but there were fewer people, too, and even fewer who fancied a glass of wine from time to time. Today's wine consumer would most likely spit out the wines produced then because the quality was certainly lacking. Unless there was absolutely nothing else to drink and you had observed others drink it and not die, you would try it. That was exactly the scenario many nonmetropolitan Pacific Northwest enophiles (I am using the term loosely) faced throughout Prohibition. Most folks who drink would probably try it. How much you actually drank might be a different story.

After the amendment's repeal, the appearance of legitimate sources of alcohol came about slowly. License fees had to be set, and then licenses applied for, reviewed, approved and granted. It would be March 1934 before everything was in place, and that was only if your local municipality decided to cooperate. In 1933, Hal Moore, a staffwriter for the *Oregonian* wrote a great article about alcohol levels in the new nonintoxicating beers compared to the beers made pre-Prohibition. This was before the beer hit the market, and it seems consumers were quite concerned that the 3.2 percent alcohol levels would change the flavor. The amount of alcohol that is in a beer or a wine does make a difference in the style and flavor. Whether consumers care about alcohol levels is a debated subject even today. The tone of Moore's article certainly reflected the belief that consumers were interested in the strength of the beverage they imbibed, just as they are today. Figures released by several breweries for pre-Prohibition beer reflected alcohol by weight. Pabst was only 2.93 percent, Miller 3.8 percent, Blatz 3.62 percent, Budweiser 3.84 percent and, a local favorite, Weinhard's was 3.42 percent. Even Stouts of the day were only 6 to 7 percent. The new lower-alcohol beer was not exactly all that much lower than the beer they drank before. In the western part of the Pacific Northwest, beer did not arrive until April 7, 1933. When Congress moved so quickly to approve the new nonintoxicating 3.2 percent beer, breweries were taken by surprise. To appease the Bible-thumping temperance twits, a public-relations campaign was mounted to make the public aware that the new beer was different and that somehow because of the lack of .2 to .5 percent alcohol from levels of pre-Prohibition beer, it would not intoxicate. Most producers thought it would be May or June before sales could take place, so production started slowly.

On April 3, 1933, over four hundred applications for beer sales were filed in Portland. The restaurant establishments of Il Trovatore on 225 Fifth Street and Henry Thieles at Twenty-third and Washington in Portland were the first and second licenses issued. Many cafés, such as the Green Mill out on Powell Boulevard, were including a pint of beer in any full course meal. They put out a great spread for a mere seventy–five cents, and they were selling bottles of Weinhard's for a quarter. Over at Jack Cody's Steak House on Washington, you could get a delicious broiled steak and a cold beer for half a buck.

The Start of a New Era

The End of Prohibition

January 1, 1934, ushered in the creation of the American Liquor Exchange, new federal tax levies on alcohol and a goodbye to the corporate tax. The federal government replaced old dividend and gasoline tax levies with new taxes on alcohol that would collect $470 million in new federal taxes on liquor.

By 1935, the newly formed Oregon Liquor Control Commission had issued over six thousand beer and wine sales licenses—a pretty good indicator that the alcoholic beverage industry was not the casualty of war the temperance society had wished for. It was not a good loser either. A couple of days prior to beer being sold in grocery stores, the Temperance Union announced it would boycott all grocery stores that decided to sell beer or wine. I wonder how that worked out for them. The first winery license the Oregon Liquor Control Commission issued went to Honeywood Winery in Salem.

Oregon's oldest continuously operating winery, Honeywood Winery in Salem, opened its doors in 1934. They had been operating as Columbia Distilleries for a year prior, producing fruit brandies, liqueurs and cordials. It was in 1934 when Ron Honeyman and John Wood decided to make premium wines and changed the name to Honeywood. Today, this winery makes some of the finest fruit wines in the world, and rightly so—they have the growers of the world's best berries, cherries, apples, apricots and pears in proximity to the winery. Their dry wines made from *Vitis vinifera* are also tasty.

The year 1934 was also the first year of the Verboort Sausage Festival in Oregon. The community formed in 1875, originally calling itself the Catholic Colony of Forest Grove. One of the founders, Father William Verboort, passed away in 1876, and the community changed the name to Verboort. It probably chose 1934 to create the event because it finally had some beer to go with the sausage. The inaugural event served almost two hundred pounds of sausage and ten gallons of sauerkraut. It has since grown to serve thirty thousand pounds of sausage and twenty thousand pounds of sauerkraut with more than ten thousand people attending according to figures released in 2010.

Verboort is a small town located very close to Oregon's famed Wine Hill, which was initially settled and farmed by Fredrick David and later Ernst Reuter—the first men to grow Pinot noir in Willamette Valley. The Verboort family and five other Dutch Catholic families emigrated from Holland to Wisconsin, and the harsh winters pushed them west to Oregon. Was the site selection for their community calculated to be near Willamette Valley's first vintners or was it just a coincident that it was so close to Wine Hill?

Louis Herbolt of Tualatin Valley Winery in 1934 reported to the *Oregonian* that they had purchased all the surplus grapes available in the area, and he encouraged growers to plant as much as they could. Herbolt went on to report that the 1934 vintage yielded seven thousand gallons of juice that was in tanks and fermenting with still more to be pressed. Lee Jones, the president of one of California's largest wineries, was in the area visiting, and he commented that over in New York, they were importing western sweetwater grapes and paying as much as $200 a ton. In New York, they used that variety to make sparkling wines. The Upland Winery in Sunnyside, Washington, also reported making seven thousand gallons of wine from its ninety acres of vines that same year. So it seems that plenty of grapevines survived Prohibition in both Oregon and Washington.

In 1937, there were forty-two wineries operating in Washington. This same year, the famed viticulture scientist Walter Clore started working at the Irrigated Agriculture Research Extension Center about five miles outside Prosser, Washington. Without the efforts of that center, it is doubtful Washington State would be the grape-producing superpower that it is today. Many consider Dr. Clore the grandfather of the Washington wine industry. His lifelong contributions to further the culture of superior-quality grapes have certainly earned him that title. Washington is our country's second-largest producer of wine grapes. That goal was clearly in the minds of many of the grape growers there early on.

Yakima started their Grape Growers Union back in 1923, and by 1930, they were producing almost four thousand tons of grapes. The Washington Wine Producers Association formed in 1935, and it brought together all the big players in the Puget Sound area. By 1938, the state's wine production reached almost 2 million gallons. Talk about going from nothing to something in no time. Those figures are impressive, especially from a location where freezes kill all the vines on a regular basis and irrigation is necessary. That same year, Pommerelle Winery acquired shares in the National Wine Company—two of the areas earliest and biggest producers. This partnership would eventually evolve into the Chateau St. Michelle winery.

Oregon's wine beginnings after the repeal of Prohibition were on a scale much smaller than that of its neighbor to the north. Around the same time in 1938, there were twenty-eight wineries in Oregon. In southern Oregon, one descendant (Adolph) of the pioneering wine family the Doerners started making a red table wine, a blend of several varieties at Doerner Winery. It sold well locally, allowing the winery to remain open until 1965.

Over in Walla Walla (well actually a little to the south of the Oregon-Washington border in Milton-Freewater to be exact) by 1940, there were over two hundred Italian gardeners who resided in the area. Among ethnic groups, the Italian, Swiss and German immigrants made a lot of homemade wine. Bert Pesciallo's father provided many of the grapes that the Italians used to make their wine. Bert had a winery he began in 1950 called Blue Mountain Vineyards in Milton Freewater, Oregon, growing mostly Black Prince grapes. In 1955, a freeze killed his vines all the way to the roots, much like the famous Walla Walla freeze of 1883. Blue Mountain closed its doors in 1955 because Bert had grown tired of the freezes that came along every few years, causing the vintners to start all over again. Bert would be the last commercial winery out there until Gary Figgins opened his doors at Leonetti Cellars in 1977.

In Washington, several growers expanded grape production during Prohibition. Rudolph Werberger emigrated from Germany at the turn of the century to Washington but left in 1904 to work with his brother's wholesale wine and liquor business in St. Louis. He returned to Puget Sound in 1918 and planted one thousand cuttings, mostly Island Belle and White Diamond, along Pickering Pass just south of Stretch Island. William Bridgman at Upland expanded plantings during Prohibition, even experimenting with Pinot noir as early as the 1930s, when Erich Steenborg came aboard. Between plantings in Walla Walla, the Yakima Valley and around the Sound when the repeal of Prohibition happened, Washington

State was ready to satisfy the needs of the state's wine drinkers much better than their neighbors to the south were. Well at least, that is what it looked like on paper. Those southern neighbors who drank wine (and let's be clear—we are talking about Oregonians) tended to embrace the resourcefulness of a more grassroots effort regarding fermentation. They kept a pretty tight lid on who knew about where and how they came by their grapes. Even today, Oregon's number-one cash crop is cultivated and distributed in the same clandestine manner.

The strong influence of Protestant religion has dictated strict moral conduct from the days of Jason Lee at the beginning of settlement in Oregon. Those circumstances created a need for a more clandestine approach for Willamette Valley residents to obtain their alcohol. When the *Oregonian* did a huge article in 1904 about Reuter and the dozens of other winemakers in the Chehalem Mountains, it led the story with how much the local temperance supporters disapproved of Reuter's winemaking. The same article mentioned that his wines were rarely bottled. Instead, the bulk of each vintage was purchased in kegs, stored and consumed in people's homes. This practice continued in many parts of Oregon all the way into the sixties. It was not just the Pacific Northwest where peer pressure from community churches set the tone for public-drinking habits. In rural areas all over the United States, if the church community could not put enough pressure on politicians to keep things dry, it would turn its efforts to berating and casting guilt on all those who chose to imbibe. The social stigma in rural areas bolstered a predilection for clandestine measures to be taken by those who appreciated the virtue of drink for years after Prohibition ended.

Choices of what we could eat or drink and our knowledge of these choices increased considerably due to the expansion of radio and the ability to listen to radio in the car or in the home. Product makers became advertisers on a completely different level, and the power of radio programming sponsorship drove the market until visual broadcasts could convey scenes of people experiencing the products. That development changed the conception of food products in a way that is hard to fully understand by people who came into this world after television was invented.

Food as entertainment found a home in the new technology broadcast television when, in 1946, Portland native James Beard hosted the first network television cooking show, *I Love to Eat*, a fifteen-minute show that appeared on Friday nights on NBC. Beard was central to the establishment of a gourmet American food identity. Today in culinary, there is no award more prestigious than the coveted James Beard Award, and many a chef has toiled to a point of ruin attempting to obtain one. Before radio, movies and television, food and dining were the major sources of daily entertainment since before the invention of fire.

The war changed everything. Culinary conditions (rationing of food supplies so soldiers could be fed) for the average household in World War II quickly matured the reasoning abilities of most Americans, as displayed in a public announcement printed in the *Oregonian*. This article featured recipes from around the world, pointing out that the food they sent to starving people in other countries to help with the war effort went to friends and foes alike. The announcement goes on to say that "it makes us realize how much we wasted in the days of plenty before the war." That is a strong statement, considering the times of plenty before the war was the Great Depression. The following recipe for sweet potato zimes came from Palestine and utilizes one of Oregon's most important crops from that era—prunes.

Sweet Potato and Prune Zimes

1 pound prunes, soaked overnight in 3 cups water (left over red
    wine would also be good)
1 beef brisket
5 medium sweet potatoes, pared, diced, salted and peppered
1 cup sugar (not necessary if red wine is used)
1 tablespoon lemon juice

Place prunes, liquid and brisket in a kettle and braise over a slow fire for 1½ hours, until brisket is tender. Remove brisket and prunes. Add sweet potatoes to broth. Place brisket and prunes on top. Add sugar, lemon juice, salt and pepper to taste. Cover kettle and return to a 350-degree oven. Cook until sweet potatoes are soft and meat is browned. Serve with gravy.

The prune-to-brisket ratio seemed a little high, but the rationing of beef made people create textures and flavors to extend the volume of whatever beef they had. This recipe does a very good job of that. The copious amount of sugar is not unusual (adding sugar to sweet potatoes is unnecessary, as the natural sugar in the potato is plenty.) Back then, I am not sure if Palestine was considered a friend or foe, not so much different than today. In all my years in culinary, I have never seen a combination of brisket, sweet potatoes and prunes. In 1946, most restaurants served a traditional board of fare similar to what was on the menu at Huber's restaurant.

It might seem interesting that a turkey drumstick, which sold for $1.35, was more expensive than prime rib of beef at $1.00, but Huber's was nationally known for its turkey. Oregonians had access to some of the freshest turkeys on the West Coast. Before vineyards covered the hills of McMinnville and Dundee and many other parts of the Willamette Valley, turkeys were a popular commodity, and farming turkeys was a viable business.

POPULARITY OF FINE DINING

Fine dining started to gain popularity in the Pacific Northwest in the early 1950s, mostly due to the GI Bill and VA home loans. All veterans returning home from the war had the ability to buy a house and go to college. That benefit allowed a record number of recent college graduates to obtain incomes not previously seen in this country. Also during the war, many women came out of the house and started working. When the men came home, not only did many of those women continue working, but many also realized that higher education brought higher pay. It was a time of prosperity that had not been seen in this country for several decades.

Once liquor by the glass was approved for sale in Puget Sound restaurants, fine-dining establishments started opening at a rapid pace in downtown Seattle. Victor Rosellini's famous 410, then the 610 and Rosellini's Other Place were bastions of epicurean delights. Peter Canlis knew the meaning of location, location, location when he opened his place high above Lake Washington on Aurora Boulevard. Canlis has a view so stunning that when combined with sophisticated innovative cuisine, it creates an experience of timeless elegance you will remember forever.

No city restaurant scene is complete without a steakhouse that can deliver the steak so good you would want it as your last meal. Jim Ward must have had that mission in mind when he opened El Gaucho, another dining experience one can still enjoy today not only in Seattle but also in Portland.

Chapter Thirteen

The Second California Invasion

Northwest Wine Regions Develop

D epending on whom you ask, Burgundy is probably the most revered wine region worldwide, although some prefer Bordeaux. Viticulture there dates back to the second century, and by the middle of the fifth century, it was receiving critical acclaim. The great historian St. Gregory of Tours compared the wines of Burgundy to the cult Roman wine Falernian, which is made from my favorite Italian variety, Aglianico. I find it utterly amazing that in less than a century, Oregon winemakers have been able to produce wines from Pinot noir grapes that rival (and sometimes compete and win) in international competitions against the wines from Burgundy. Especially since the Pinot noir grape is not known for its ease of cultivation. It is also incomprehensible that of the hundreds of grape varieties that Pacific Northwest viticulturists experimented with, no one attempted to grow Pinot noir before 1961.

Peter Britt reportedly experimented with over eight hundred varieties of grapes. Adolph Reuter of Forest Grove and August Aufranc of Salem both claimed in the 1901 Oregon Agricultural Experiment Station, Bulletin 66, that they grew red Burgundy (Pinot noir).

Debating who grew Pinot noir first in Oregon is an argument that continues to drag on, but truth be told, most consumers could care less. They just want to drink great wine. However, it does not seem plausible that, of all the regions known for fine wine, no one decided to replicate the wines of Burgundy here in the Pacific Northwest until the 1960s. Especially since the climate is very similar to that of Burgundy, France. Sure, maybe most people who tried found cultivating Pinot noir challenging. Then, it would be a given that they might not have been so proud of how the wines turned out, but there are too many references to the contrary to say Oregon's Pinot noir history started with the second California invasion of winemakers coming out of the reputable and well-known University of California–Davis (aka UC–Davis) in the 1960s.

Richard Sommer, (aka Richard Sommers) was talking about growing grapes in the cool climate of Oregon in the 1950s while he was at UC Davis. A few years later—some reports say 1960, others 1961—he made it to Roseburg and found a site, which became Hillcrest Vineyards. Those years were the lowest dip the Oregon wine industry had ever seen, with only six wineries operating in the state. By 1967, Hillcrest Vineyards and Honeywood

Top left: Richard Sommer, 1967. *Right*: Myron Redford, circa 1960s. *Bottom left*: portrait of Adam Doerner. *Middle and right*: Richard Sommer at Hillcrest Vineyards, June 1967. *Photos courtesy of Dyson DeMara.*

Barrels at Hillcrest Vineyard. *Photo courtesy of Dyson DeMara.*

Richard Sommer at Hillcrest Vineyards, 1967. *Photo courtesy of Dyson DeMara.*

wines were available at the gourmet wine shop inside Meier & Frank, the Pacific Northwest's equivalent to Macy's back then. Sommer made a few wines that national critics proclaimed palatable. Leon D. Adams, a noted wine writer, visited Hillcrest Vineyards and proclaimed Sommer's Riesling to be balanced with true Riesling aroma.

Despite a quality education in enology, Sommer went through a trial-and-error period. One of them included his first shipment of Riesling to Jake's Famous Crawfish in 1971. This placement was urged by the distributor, Henny-Hinsdale, and when Fred Delkin, the owner of Jake's, gave the go ahead, the wine was delivered on time. Delkin got a call from Henny. He had called to ask if he had tasted the wine, and Delkin had not. Henny urged him to try the wine immediately. After popping the cork on one, Delkin discovered the wine tasted like turpentine (Mr. Delkin's descriptor), or to be more exact, Riesling mixed with oak and Scotch.

Sommer, in his haste (and maybe with a little too much frugality), decided to store the Riesling in oak vats purchased from Hood River Distillers, which had previously held imported Scotch. The containers were probably sold without disclosure. Distillers at the time would not have contributed to the success of a winery. Their customer base was strong, and they did not need

Richard Sommer at a wine tasting, 1972. *Photo courtesy of Dyson DeMara.*

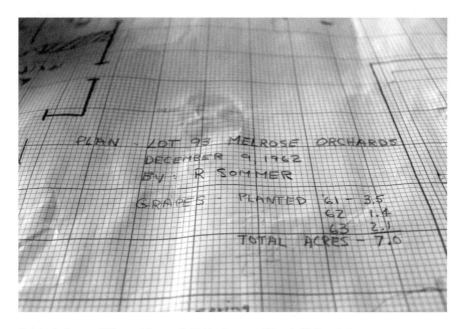

Original plans at Hillcrest Vineyard, 1962. *Courtesy of Pamela Heiligenthal.*

Hillcrest Vineyard 1970 Cabernet Sauvignon. *Courtesy of Pamela Heiligenthal.*

JAKE'S WINE LIST

These are our personal selections to best complement our menu. Each represents an outstanding vintage for its price.

HOUSE WINE

Mountain White or Mountain Red
By the glass .... .65
Small Carafe (for 1 or 2) 1.25
Large Carafe (for 2 or 4) 2.00
Full Litre (for 4 or 6) 2.75

WHITE WINES — Domestic

	tenth	fifth
Bjelland Johannisberger Reisling	1.75	3.00
(Oregon's own and a match for California!)		
Sebastiani Green Hungarian		
(Dry yet quite light and smooth, a Califronia exclusive)	1.80	3.50
Charles Krug Chenin Blanc		
(Medium dry, superb with Bouillabaise, Coquille)	1.80	3.50
Souverain Pinot Chardonnay		
(California classic, best of the region, very dry)		6.00

WHITE WINES — Imported

Alsatian selections — unusual values from the French province of Alsace, bordering on the better known Rhine wine districts of Germany.

Hugel Alsatian Pinot Blanc (Full dry wine that fits salmon perfectly)	2.50	4.75
Josmeyer Alsatian Riesling (Very dry for its type, yet light, best with shellfish)	2.75	5.00
Hugel Gewurztraminer (Spicy flavor, medium dry, try with smoked salmon)	3.50	6.00

Joseph Drouhin bottlings — in our estimation as fine a shipper as graces the wine lists of France. The name is synonymous with ultimate quality in each type offered.

Drouhin Chablis 1969. (Dry, yet full, superb with oysters)	3.50	6.00
Drouhin Pouilly Fuisse 1969 (French classic with fish, our best value)	3.00	5.25
Anheuser & Fehrs Liebfraumilch (Reknowned German import, smooth and light)	2.75	5.00

ROSE'

Portugal produces the world's best rose's for the price, known for their imaginative bottle shapes. Mateus still rose'

(Dry, full bodied, goes with everything)	2.00	3.85
Rose' Bela (Sweeter, a favorite with the ladies, yet light) 6-oz.	1.95	2.85

RED

Souverain Burgundy (Finest moderately priced California red available)		3.75
Joseph Drouhin Beaujolais Villages '69 (Best of its type, light and dry yet with body)	2.75	5.00

SPARKLING

DuValle Cold Duck (bubbling blend of red and white wines)	3.75
DuValle Extra Dry California Champagne (modest yet good)	3.85

From France — we have selected the finest imported champagne from one of the world's most prestigious producers, considered to have no equal.

Taittinger N.V. (Dry, exquisitely smooth)	11.75
Taittinger Comtesse (Simply, an experience)	23.00

SPECIAL CELLARS

For the final touch on your special occasion, or simply to allow you to sample the last squeeze in the grape presser's art, we present a selection of the world's leading vintages that set the standards for every wine producer.

Drouhin Chassagne-Montrachet '69 (Rich, fruity, yet very dry white burgundy from France's Cote de Beaune)	12.75
Piesporter Goldtrockenauslese '69 (Light, delicate medium dry Moselle from Germany)	11.00
Bernkasteler Doktor Wwe. Thanisch '69 (Most famous Moselle, fresh and elegant, light yet rich)	22.00
Chateau Haut-Brion premiers crus classe' '64 (World's finest bordeaux, rich and fruity, yet dry)	20.00
Joseph Drouhin Clos de la Roche '64 (Great burgundy from a great year, very full)	15.50

AFTER DINNER DRINKS

JAKE'S FAMOUS CRAWTINI	1.25
APRICOT FLEECE (Fleecy Creme d'menthe, Apricot Brandy Cream)	1.50
THE RUSTIC CLAW (For Scotch Drinker . . . on the rocks)	1.25

Jake's Crawfish wine list, circa 1971, Portland, Oregon. *Courtesy of Fred Delkin.*

any winemaking California hippies cutting into it. Who knows, maybe it was just an honest mistake and a misunderstanding. The show went on when new wine arrived and passed the famous "Jake's test," in which Delkin approved. Jake's Famous Crawfish was the only restaurant in Oregon selling an Oregon Riesling. The modern era of Oregon wine sold in restaurants started with that transaction.

These days, current proprietor, Dyson Demara, continues the tradition of innovation at Hillcrest, creating unique proprietary red blends and distinctive late harvest Rieslings and Gewürztraminer, as well as European-styled Chardonnay. Hillcrest continues to produce wines that reflect the quality Oregon is famous for.

Going back to UC–Davis in 1962, there were four guys in the enology program—Bill Fuller, David Lett, Charles Coury and Bruno Filone. Three of the four headed to Oregon, starting with Charles Coury in 1965 and

Hillcrest Vineyards owner and winemaker Dyson DeMara, 2013. *Courtesy of Pamela Heiligenthal.*

followed by David Lett and eventually Bill Fuller. Coury established his vineyard in Forest Grove at the northern part of Willamette Valley on Reuter's former site. They came chasing the same cool climate grape-growing dream as Richard Sommer, just reaching further north of the Willamette Valley.

Soon after Coury arrived, David Lett headed to Oregon, too, establishing Eyrie Vineyards in 1967. Eyrie Vineyards is an Oregon wine institution, and the Letts are a great family. David Lett, through his tireless efforts to make fantastic wines, was always there for anyone who wanted to know how to grow grapes in Oregon. David Lett's efforts in keeping land-use laws in favor of grape growers and agriculture in general were monumental, and to this day, those accomplishments define why viticulture in Oregon is as progressive as it is through exclusive farm-use zoning regulations. Mr. Lett certainly earned his moniker of "Papa Pinot." Jason Lett, David's son, took over for his father five years ago and has done a fantastic job at putting his mark on the wines and running the winery. Jason's mother, Diana, has also contributed to the success of the winery including preserving the historical significance of that venerable wine institution.

David Lett had a connection with Craig Broadley, the man who made my Oregon epiphany wine. Mr. Lett and Mr. Broadley had something in

NEWBERG GRAPHIC, THURSDAY, FEB. 16, 1967, SEC. 2, Pages 1 to 6

Purchase Old Blanchard Place

DAVID AND DIANA LETT, who recently purchased the John Marner (former Everett Blanchard) place in Dundee, pause for a moment with their European wine grape rootings. The Letts plans on removing prunes from the 20 acre farm and putting in quality wine grapes. Lett has a degree in food technology and has been looking for several years for a favorite spot to grow grapes. Dundee should be perfect, he feels.

David Lett purchased the John Marner (former Everett Blanchard) place in Dundee with plans to remove prunes from the twenty-acre farm and put in quality wine grapes (February 16, 1967). *Courtesy Newberg Graphic Farm News.*

The Ponzi family, *from left to right*: Maria, Nancy, Luisa, Michael and Dick. *Courtesy of Ponzi Vineyards.*

Dick and Nancy Ponzi in the vineyard, circa early 1970s. *Courtesy of Ponzi Vineyards.*

Dick Ponzi in the vineyard, circa early 1970s. *Courtesy of Ponzi Vineyards.*

common before either of them became winemakers—they both sold books. Broadley was the owner of the famous San Francisco bookstore City Lights Books, known as the Beat poets' hangout on Columbus Boulevard. These days, Craig Broadley produces some of the finest Pinot noir made in Oregon. His 1987 Pinot noir was the first Oregon wine I fell in love with. That vintage was spectacular. It danced across my palate with the gait of a lover you will never forget.

I was eager to talk to Mr. Broadley after finding out that he and David Lett were contemporaries in two different occupations. They both sold books and then made wine. Lett supplemented his income selling college books while waiting for his vines to reach the maturity level to make a great bottle of wine. When Broadley came to Oregon looking for a site, he wanted to learn as much as he could. His objective was to find a great site and talk to all the current players. About that visit Craig said, "Lett was always available and helped anyone he could," something that could not be said for some of the other Oregon wine pioneers from the second California invasion, such as Coury and Sommer. When interviewing Nancy Ponzi, she echoed the same sentiment. When asked if she ever imagined the industry would evolve to what it is today, Nancy replied, "No! I think people have to go back to the

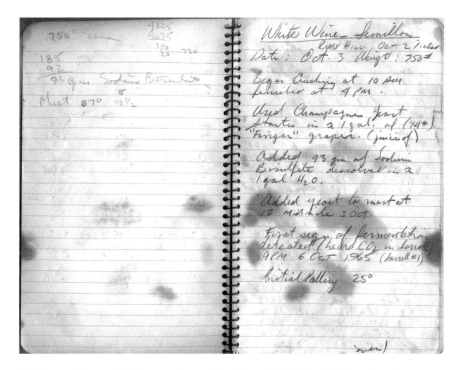

This image shows an inside page of a notebook kept by Dick Erath during the early years of his winemaking career. *Courtesy of Erath Winery and Dick Erath, 1965.*

mindset of the '60s, and this is true of the Eraths, the Letts to some extent—we were looking for an alternate lifestyle. We had no concept of a business. The person who did have a vision was Charles Coury. I always point this out because he was the one that really knew it would be possible, was thinking twenty years ahead and really set the tone for what was to come." When asked if Coury was the go-to person to get answers about the wine business, Nancy responded, "No, he was not a very social person. Dick Ponzi (maker of the first Oregon Pinot noir I ever tasted) and Dick Erath were the friendly people, continually willing to share their information and knowledge." Erath's influence with Jim Maresh and Don Lange is a testament to his involvement in the industry at every level. Dick Ponzi lived and breathed hospitality, creating Bridgeport Brewing, Dundee Bistro and Ponzi Wine Bar.

Coury sold his first Pinot noir in 1972. Lett also sold a wine that same year called Oregon Spring Wine. Although it was not labeled Pinot noir, it makes no difference. If they both came to market the same year what is the point of contention? The *Oregonian* reported Coury brought his first Pinot

This wine label from Erath Vineyards describes its estate-bottled 1976 appellation Willamette Valley white Riesling Oregon table wine. *Courtesy of Erath Winery and Dick Erath.*

noir to market in 1972. In an interview with Dan Berger from 1976, David Lett would not divulge what grapes besides Pinot noir were in the Oregon Spring Wine, but he admitted there is a little Muscat Ottonel in the mix, an odd choice to add to a young Pinot noir and just an interesting side note for the super wine geeks.

On the other side of the tale is the Charles Coury and the city of Forest Grove, Oregon side of the story and, to a degree, the David Hill Winery story. Adolph Reuter's plot, Wine Hill (aka David Hill) in Forest Grove, was sold in 1934 and has changed hands several times in between. Now owned and operated by Milan Stoyanov and his lovely wife, Jean, the winery is appropriately named David Hill. They have been stalwart supporters of the Oregon wine industry without being drawn into the fray about who has the oldest Pinot noir vines in the Willamette Valley.

In no way am I trying to detract from the fact that Eyrie Vineyards and David Hill make some great wine. However, the debate about who among those in the second California invasion of Oregon winemakers was first to plant Pinot noir is a moot point.

Since Reuter grew and sold Pinot noir wines on Wine Hill in Forest Grove prior to Prohibition, and Bridgman at Upland in Washington is on record

Bill Fuller, Tualatin Vineyards, Forest Grove, Oregon, 1978. Unknown photographer. *Courtesy of Fred Delkin.*

saying he made Burgundy (Pinot noir) prior to 1954, (which is backed up by several other references of others growing Pinot noir all over the Pacific Northwest prior to the mid-1960s, such as August Aufranc in Salem and Fredrick David of Forest Grove, who also served as Reuter's mentor), first in Oregon has to go to someone prior to Prohibition.

Heading south, the southern Oregon wine institution Valley View Vineyards was established in 1854 by Peter Britt and then resurrected by Frank Wisnovsky in 1971. Wisnovsky made his first two vintages at Tualatin Vineyards. This vineyard in Willamette Valley has gone through the same progression of owners as of late, beginning with Bill Fuller who bought the former strawberry farm in the 1970s and produced a run of award-winning wines through 1997. The 1980 Pinot noir and 1981 Chardonnay took double gold and "Best of Show" trophies at London's prestigious international judging in 1984. The Queen of England presented the trophies. With Lett winning the 1979 Gault-Millau French Wine Olympiades for his 1975 Pinot noir and Fuller's accolades in 1984, Oregon wine was set to capture the adoration of enophiles who had previously consumed Pinot noir only from Burgundy and, rarely, from Germany.

On a larger scale, anyone with any sense would ascertain the ground and atmosphere that is perfect for growing Pinot noir could also nurture many other varietals, and so an industry began. California hippies seeking an alternative lifestyle started showing up in droves. The rise in demand for table wines in the 1950s and '60s in the United States skyrocketed, and by 1965, table wines were outselling desert wines. Many native sons of the Pacific Northwest also decided to join the fray by starting vineyards of their own. Bjelland, Redford, Erath, Adelsheim, Ponzi, Fuller, Sokol-Blosser, Maresh, Arterberry, Vuylsteke, Campbell, Shafer, Troon, Girardet and a host of other families decide to try their hands at viticulture in Oregon, and only a few of those names have left the business to enter retirement or pursue other interests. The rest have all handed the reins to the next generation. Dick and Nancy Ponzi, who, in 1969, purchased a house three miles from the Ponzi site, confidently turned over the winemaking duties to their daughter Luisa, who has done her parents and the Willamette Valley proud with the excellent wines she makes year after year. Joe and Pat Campbell certainly imbued a sense of "get 'er done" in their son, Adam Campbell because he does, and his results are spectacular. The Oregon wine industry has grown quite a bit since the early '60s, as it is now the fourth-largest wine producer in the United States.

In 1963, there were six wineries in existence, which increased to thirteen in '73. Oregon's surge in new vineyard plantings in the early '70s started to slow by the middle of the decade, as investors decided to pull back on supporting the Oregon wine industry during the recession in 1975. But by '78, things started to pick up again, and by the early '80s, there were forty-one wineries. And no matter how bad it got, whether it was subzero temperatures in Washington wiping out whole vineyards or severe damage to the crops from birds in Oregon, Pacific Northwest vintners decided they were in this for the long haul. They persevered. In 1976, Myron Redford built his Amity Vineyards and made his first wine, a Pinot noir nouveau. By 1977, Bill Blosser and his wife, Susan Sokol-Blosser, crushed their first vintage, as did Pat and Joe Campbell at Elk Cove.

In the northeastern part of the United States, where California wines struggled to compete with European wines, Oregon and Washington wines started to become a familiar sight on store shelves. The year 1986 brought superstar winemaker Ken Wright onto the scene with the opening of Panther Creek in McMinnville, Oregon. The next year, Mike Wetzel (the brother-in-law of acclaimed wine critic Robert Parker) plants Beaux Frères. The inaugural International Pinot Noir Celebration (IPNC) was held in McMinnville that year, too, a celebration now twenty-seven years running. The celebration draws international attention and producers from as far as New Zealand.

Around the same time, Joe Dobbes returned from working in Europe and started at Elk Cove. Joe eventually will go on to become one of the most innovative and successful winemakers in Oregon with three labels of his own and a custom crush facility that produces over 100,000 cases a year for some very high-profile clients.

In 1988, Domaine Drouhin from Burgundy (in an if-you-can't-beat-them-join-them move) started to plant the 225-acre parcel it bought in the Willamette Valley the previous year. Drouhin Oregon was the first to plant Pinot noir Dijon clones grafted onto phylloxera-resistant rootstock using high-density spacing—a first in Oregon viticulture.

In 1989, the greatest grape grower in the Willamette Valley, Dick Shea, planted one hundred acres near Chehalem Creek with the intent of becoming a grower, only to realize he'd make his own wine too. The Wine Spectator scored ninety-five points for his 2004 Pinot noir, placing him on the best winemaker in Oregon list. That is an impressive accomplishment for a guy who spent half his life on Wall Street proving Sinatra wasn't wrong: "If you can make it in New York, you can make it anywhere." And let that be a lesson to all you rednecks who denigrate city slickers from New York; they could come to your neck of the woods and become cock of the walk.

Over the next decade, the Pacific Northwest wine industry expanded at an ever-increasing pace. Biodynamic, organic and sustainable started to become the distinguishing identities between Oregon and the rest of the West Coast wine producers. In 1991, King Estate was established and became

Dick and Deirdre Shea, Shea Wine Cellars & Vineyard, 2013. *Courtesy of Pamela Heiligenthal.*

the largest organic vineyard in Oregon. Earl and Hilda Jones established Abacela in 1995, planting the first Tempranillo vines in Oregon. Over the next fifteen years, the number of wineries in Oregon rises to over 400, and Washington boasted it was home to an incredible 780 wineries.

WASHINGTON STATE

In November 1955, a devastating freeze in Washington killed many of the vines. The devastation was so bad that it was named the Black Frost of '55.

For many viticulturists, growing grapes started to lose its commercial appeal, and by 1958, there were only nine Washington wineries still in operation. Today, Washington is the second-largest wine producer in America, with only California exceeding production, producing high-quality Cabernet Sauvignon, Merlot, Syrah, Chardonnay and Riesling. In the 1960s and '70s, the Washington wine industry followed a different path from its Oregon neighbor's—not only were vineyards growing different grapes, but true to form, they did it with a lot of organization through grower associations. One unique but odd observation about the wine industry reveals operating in an organized manner has nothing to do with how good the wine turns out. Often, it is the small family-owned and operated wineries in the Pacific Northwest that garner the highest critical acclaim, but not always. Columbia Crest, Willamette Valley Vineyards, Chateau St. Michelle and King Estate, to name some of the larger producers, have all had their share of critically acclaimed wines, too.

In 1966, noted wine author Leon Adams visited Yakima Valley and was impressed with Grenache samples. Vic Allison planted Grenache for the National Wine Company (NAWICO) in Columbia Valley in Washington State back in 1951, a few years before NAWICO merged with Pommerelle to become the American Wine Growers (AWG). Adams suggested to Allison that Washington vintners should make vinifera wines on a commercial scale based on his evaluation of the samples he tasted. The grapes of success conveniently were planted somehow in sync with the new middle-classes desire for table wine.

Washington's early fine-wine business model was propelled by a woman; an unusual occurrence in the 1960s. Even more unusual was the fact that Martha Niblack was a southern Baptist woman from Mississippi who did not drink. She arrived in the Pacific Northwest in 1942 to work at the Hanford Nuclear Facility. In 1957, Martha moved to Renton and began working for the Buttnick family, who owned Old West Wines. She was an ambitious woman, who rose through the ranks believing that "wine was a part of gracious living" and that "people want that touch of class, that touch of glamour associated with wine." Niblack once visited Charles Krug winery in Napa and thought, "That is what a winery should be." With Krug in mind, Chateau Merryl was conceived by Niblack for Old West Wines to capitalize on the desire to get wine to those who were seeking that little bit of class, a moment of glamour. Niblack's attempts at gaining placements at Safeway and a need to facilitate the public's desire to class it up a bit with a bottle of wine on the dinner table caught the attention of Vic Allison.

Stealing Niblack's concept, American Wine Growers debuted its Chateau St. Michelle brand. Vic Allison also influenced Safeway buyers to keep Chateau Merryl off the shelves. Expansion plans did not materialize to improve wine-production quality and marketing efforts. Chateau Merryl, with all its innovation and ambition, did not last long enough to give wine enthusiasts what they were seeking. Chateau Merryl and Old West Wines last vintage was in 1969. However, Martha Niblack's influence changed the conception of what Washington wine could be forever.

The year 1969 also happened to be the same year the Washington state legislature passed State Bill 100, also called the California Wine Bill. The legislature effectively leveled the playing field for out-of-state wineries to sell their wines in Washington just as in-state wineries did. Without pricing protection competition, Washington wineries started to lose market share quickly. Washington grape growers only needed to taste the wines Dr. Walter Clore was making at the irrigation experimental station in Prosser to prove that Washington wine could compete on an international level.

From 1971 to 1984, Joel Klein, winemaker for Chateau Ste. Michelle, advocated the use of mechanical pickers for fine-wine grapes. It was one of the most influential and innovative logistical contributions to the industry, according to Dr. Wade Wolf, owner of Thurston-Wolfe Winery in Prosser, Washington. Although juice companies had been using mechanical pickers for years in eastern Washington with great success, they were still frowned on across the nation by wine producers who preferred the gentle and labor-intensive method of handpicking and hand sorting. By 1974, Chateau St. Michelle's annual production accounted for 75 percent of all Washington wine. Thanks to Joel Klein's advocacy for mechanical pickers, the winery got the grapes in quickly, cleanly and, most importantly, in pristine condition.

The 1980s brought a lot of national attention as American consumers developed a palate for Pacific Northwest wines. In 1983, Columbia Crest, an eighteen-thousand-acre farm in Tri-Cities, Washington, was created in step with Washington's "bigger is better" plan. By 1985, ten of the wines on the Wine Spectator's prestigious "Top 100 List" were from Washington State. Meanwhile in Hillsboro, Oregon, Oak Knoll's Ron Vuylsteke was well on his way to become the big daddy of American fruit wines, enabling his brand to capture national attention and paving the way for his sweet white Niagara, which is still a huge success, especially around the midwestern states.

The Columbia Gorge's place in wine history may have been saved in 1987, when Lonnie Wright started to nurse Washington's oldest Zinfandel vines back to life at what would become The Pines 1852 Vineyard and

Winery. Another subzero freeze hit eastern Washington in 1996, lasting five days with six inches of snow cover. It was the most devastating weather in forty-six years.

Continuing the Pacific Northwest wine industry's transformation to what it has become today there are many changes on the horizon. The new millennium ushered in a new era of winemakers operating from suburban (and even city) wineries to provide libations for a newer wine consumer—something called the millennial. Among that group are chefs and sommeliers who have never worked in a restaurant or sold a bottle of wine. Established wine media began to struggle as knowledgeable wine writers aged and disappeared. The proliferation of wine blogging started to blur the lines of integrity, and separating wine journalism from wine infotainment has become almost impossible. This development has forced mainstream media writers who already have jobs to start blogs to keep pace with the present "wine bloggers" who will say anything (mostly in 140 characters or less) for a free bottle of wine.

One thing is certain: every wine lover should relish in the glory of the wines currently produced in the Pacific Northwest. We have some of the best Bordeaux and Burgundy-like growing regions up here offering all consumers with a taste for fine wine a choice of either style. Dollar for dollar, the Pacific Northwest produces some of the best wine values in the world when you consider the quality-to-price ratio. Considering the best Bordeaux wines will fetch thousands per bottle (the same can be said for Burgundy), the best Oregon Pinot noir rarely breaks the $100 threshold. Up in Washington State, where Bordeaux style wines dominate, a couple c-notes will get you the best with enough change to get a bottle of their best white wine too. Oregon's best white wines are as inexpensive as they are varied—Pinot gris, Chardonnay, Pinot blanc, Sauvignon blanc, Semillon, Riesling, Viognier Gewürztraminer, Muller-Thurgau, just to name a few—and all are obtainable in good to excellent examples for under $20 a bottle. Oregon and Washington State have parlayed their wine production into industries with billions of dollars a year affecting the states economies.

Continuation of the Pacific Northwest's rise to superstar status among the world's wine producing regions will require innovation in areas never conceived before. For the eastern part of Washington, protecting vine trunks during the winter months through insulation and developing a system to divert warm water to warm the roots should be on the horizon. It might be expensive, but so is ripping out vines after a hard freeze. Installing pipes for circulating warm water to the vine roots in winter would be an advantage and should not be too difficult to connect to the existing irrigation systems. Most of those vineyards have already contemplated retooling to provide solar-heated water to control root temperatures. Oregon winemakers are making strides toward improvement in all areas of viticulture and enology and moving forward at breakneck speed. Throughout the Pacific Northwest, winemakers need to keep the goal in mind to make the best wines they can and ask for a reasonable return on their investment. Now on to more about Pacific Northwest food, because after all, the food was always here—it just took a while for the wines to catch up.

Chapter Fourteen

Pacific Northwest's Rise to Culinary Stardom

D igital media has changed the exchange of information to a degree that what we know and hope to know is limitless. I am not saying that learning new things in the past had a finite limit but time dictated how much information one could gather. Today, we are still in the infancy of information evolution. However, no matter how far we move forward in technology and the exchange of information, until we can manipulate the molecular structure of matter (Star Trek–replicator style), our subsistence will still depend on what we can farm, biologically raise or clone.

Just the idea of synthetic food and drink is somewhat appalling to me, and I am not really sure why. While nourishing ourselves we experience smells, sounds and tastes, and those senses are stored in our memory, providing a reference for us to call on each and every time we eat. The evolution of those senses kept us alive by reminding us through sight, smell and taste what was poisonous. Figuring out what will kill us is not quite that easy anymore.

There are several influential back-to-basic food movements popular today that are trying to make consumers aware of the options for ingesting healthier choices. They go by many different names, including organic, biodynamic, locavore, farm to table, slow food and raw food/live food, and the common thread that creates a singularity of mission among them is getting back to what was done with food prior to chemicals, mass processing, bioengineering and not being afraid to get your hands dirty. If you research what is going on in food science and bioengineering you will adopt the phrase, "The more you know the more you will grow." Take my word on that one. Truly, words

Organically grown vegetables from the Pacific Northwest. *Courtesy of Pamela Heiligenthal.*

to live or die by, you make the choice. This quote, taken from the *Portland Mercury*, from Greg Higgins echoes my inspiration for writing this book about the bounty offered to the Pacific Northwest culinarians who commit to create:

> *The range of ingredients in Oregon eclipses even what is available in the Napa and Sonoma counties of California. We have great lamb, seafood, vegetables, game meats, huckleberries and hazelnuts. The local produce is just superlative, including, of course, the salmon.*

As much as the fervor here is about the beauty and bounty of product, the clamor to be involved goes deep into wanting to provide sustenance. Culinary artisans of the Pacific Northwest craft the best from their hearts, whether it's raising vegetation from the soil, fishing for it off the coast or raising it in green pastures according to certified humane-handling guidelines. The care in how pigs, sheep, cows, bison, chickens and even their eggs are raised in the Pacific Northwest produces a near-perfect product. The chickens are so happy here they lay multicolored eggs.

Let's talk fruits and berries. When we talk about fruit, it is hard to imagine how much fruit there is here in the Pacific Northwest. Fruit wines were popular here because they provided a revenue stream from a product that might have otherwise gone to waste. The demand for those wines has waned, which is a good thing, but you can still get the best fruit wines in the world here. One thing that has changed regarding fruit consumption is people nowadays consume a lot more fruit in many different ways, most notably with savory dishes and, of course, as the ubiquitous fruit smoothie, which is now a staple offered in every mall in America and internationally, too. Rainier cherries, Skagit Valley and Mount Hood strawberries, Dilley raspberries and blueberries—I could go on forever. I won't even start on apples and pears and all the other stone fruits or nuts. If I mentioned nuts, there would have to be soup, right? I would then have to mention the oysters, clams and mussels, which would lead to Taylor Shellfish Farms, the country's largest producer of farmed shellfish. Chances are if you've eaten mussels, clams or oysters in a restaurant, you have probably consumed Taylor Shellfish Farms' products.

The Pacific Northwest seafood that for so long was only consumed fresh within a few miles from where it was harvested now arrives on the other side of the world in less than twenty-four hours. Canned fish consumption has dropped dramatically over the years as logistics improve and restaurant demand for fresh product dictated the demise of that industry. In the interior of this country, fresh seafood counters at supermarkets were next to impossible to find three decades ago. Today, you would be hard pressed not to find one even in places like Denver, Memphis or any other landlocked metropolitan area.

Beyond the raw products this region is so fortunate to have, there are many national and international influences in the form of food and beverage purveyors that originated in the Pacific Northwest. No one needs to tell you Starbucks is from Seattle (unless you just landed on this planet, and even then, I think aliens would know a tall is a small and a grande is a medium). I know this because once, while standing in line at Starbucks, I commented, "On what planet does a tall equal a small?" A very nondescript figure slouching behind me, face hidden in a hoodie said, very matter-of-factly, "Earth." On a recent trip to Melbourne, Australia, I was surprised to see a Costco on my ride from the airport to the hotel. McDonald's promotes our famous mega cheese company from the Oregon Coast—Tillamook cheese—on its burgers, and the take-and-bake pizza phenomenon Papa Murphy's started right here in Hillsboro, Oregon. Pacific Northwest beers are on the shelves everywhere, and for good reason—they are world class. Ninkasi from Eugene makes several of the best IPAs in the world. That is the picture of how a lot of the world knows the Pacific Northwest. But if you come here, you will see another world, a place where passion and innovation flow not just in the culinary field but in those of technology and music, too.

Take the Grilled Cheese Grill, whose slogan is "Come by for a taste of your childhood, unless your childhood sucked, then we'll let you have a taste of ours." They created the cheesus, two grilled cheese sandwiches with a huge burger in between. Although they have four locations, they are all food

The Grilled Cheese Grill food cart in Portland, Oregon. *Courtesy of Pamela Heiligenthal.*

The famous Original Cheesus at the Grilled Cheese Grill food cart in Portland, Oregon. *Courtesy of Pamela Heiligenthal.*

Food carts in Portland, Oregon. *Courtesy of Pamela Heiligenthal.*

cart operations. The menu of grilled cheese sandwich creations covers all the bases, with some real culinary twists. Portland was ground zero for the food cart explosion, and that fire is never likely to be put out, much to the chagrin of brick and mortar restaurants, who lament the competition from street vendors who have little overhead, enabling them to put out product for much less money.

So when was that switch flipped that propelled the Pacific Northwest to becoming one of the hottest culinary scenes in the world? What changed and why did those changes take place? It is really hard to say what exactly happened, but restaurant food changed in the 1970s. Not just in the Pacific Northwest—it happened all over the country, in most metropolitan cities. It was 1971 when Alice Waters opened Chez Panisse in Berkeley. That opening caused a lot of commotion. It was as if her place had been dropped like a rock into the sea of the American dining scene and started a ripple that turned into a tidal wave. Ambitious cooks were like surfers; they wanted to ride that tidal wave of change, and ride it they did. Jeremiah Tower came out of that kitchen and across the bay to San Francisco to open Stars around the same time Zuni Cafe opened. Moving east, one of my most influential restaurant moments was a brief stop at Mark Miller's Coyote Café in Santa Fe in 1987. In addition to the food, the décor, the staff and the ambience all represented a new era of dining. It was then and there I made the decision to return to the stove after a multiple-year hiatus. A lot of other seminal events in the culinary world took place that year. Up in Chicago, Rick Bayless and Charlie Trotter opened their restaurants, and over in New York, Daniel Boulud started at Le Cirque. Todd English, Chris Schlesinger, Jasper White and Lydia Shire in New England opened restaurants around the same time. In 1987, I was cooking at 271 Dartmouth, awarded "Best New Restaurant" in that same year by the Boston Globe. Todd English opened his first restaurant, Olives, in Boston in 1989, the same year 271 Dartmouth closed and reopened as Papa Razzi. Chef English and I worked the Spinazzola Affair side by side that fall, vying for prospective guests while promoting the new restaurants we were involved with. Papa Razzi quickly spread to six locations, and I think English has done well for himself. In the late '80s, down in D.C., Philly, Miami, Dallas, Atlanta and across the nation, cities were seeing a revival of American-trained chefs take hold and launch eateries that could excite diners. When eating becomes fun, it can be a little addictive, and you start looking for that next great experience. Add wine to the mix, and it becomes a lifestyle.

When contemplating who were the influential players in the Pacific Northwest culinary revolution, names such as Jon Rowley, Greg Higgins,

Tom Douglas, Vitaly Paley, Dave Machado, Tamara Murphy, Holly Smith, Chris Israel and Thierry Rautureau all spring to mind. All are chefs, except for Jon Rowley, who, besides being a culinarian, is the Pacific Northwest's seafood ambassador extraordinaire. Jon Rowley earned that title for revolutionizing how fish are handled through teaching commercial fishermen the economics of best product equals best price. To the benefit of the wholesale seafood industry in the Pacific Northwest, Jon Rowley's contributions exemplify passion and innovation. Rowley's ardent love of fresh (like-nobody's-ever-tasted-before) fish brought demand instantly after prospective buyers tasted the product. Jon turned his passion into a lifelong journey. This instigated relationships between buyers and sellers with getting the freshest, best-tasting seafood to consumers as the only motive. We credit Jon with facilitating Ray's Boathouse of Seattle with the first Copper River Salmon in 1983. He also brought the Olympia oyster out of jars and back to the tables of fine restaurants around the same time. Unbelievably, Pacific Northwest restaurants at the time were serving a lot of frozen fish. Another innovation was Rowley's use of refractors at produce markets to check sugar levels—a stroke of genius. What I find odd is that most chefs know what a refractor is and what it does as a tool, but they do not use them. Probably the thought never crossed their minds to utilize a tool used mostly by viticulturists to measure sugar levels on grapes to ascertain sugar levels in produce. Jon Rowley continues to make significant contributions to the Pacific Northwest culinary scene. If you attend Tamara Murphy's annual feast in a field, Burning Beast, you will probably run into him.

Greg Higgins grew up in the farming communities of upstate New York, came to Portland to open the new Heathman Hotel in 1984 and, by 1988, had conceptualized and opened B. Moloch, a bakery and pub that served gastro-pub fare before it was even called that. Greg said he had to open a bakery for the hotel because there was nowhere to get good bread and having the brewery there just made sense. Greg was one of the first to build relationships with growers. It happened out of necessity because no one was producing the products he wanted to cook with. Higgins opened in 1994 and has pleased the palates of customers and critics ever since. The following year, Chef Tony Demes came to Portland after stints with some of the best chefs in New York and opened Couvron. Tony is the only chef in America to ever achieve a perfect rating of thirty for food from the Zagat guide for both 1997 and 1998. Demes headed back to NYC in 2005 and opened Couvron NYC. After five years, Demes returned to Portland in 2010 to open Noisette. Last year, I attended a Pre-IPNC (International Pinot noir

Celebration) dinner at Noisette and was impressed. Obviously, the folks at AAA and Zagat were, too, awarding Chef Demes the only Four Diamond rating in Portland and a near perfect rating for food from Zagat.

To better understand where the Pacific Northwest's food scene is today and how we got to this point, I turned to people in the food and wine business here who have been here a lot longer than I have. What I found with my queries was that dining out in the Pacific Northwest during the 1950s, '60s and '70s was as boring as it was in the rest of the country. This quote from an interview that Greg Higgins did for the *Portland Mercury* in 2008 sums it up better than I could:

> *First thing they do, of course, in that situation is that they take you out to dinner and dine you around for a few nights to see what the competition has. Not to belittle it, but it struck me that everybody was cooking out of Gourmet magazine from like 1968 or something.*

Higgins was responding to a question about what the dining scene in Portland was like in the 1980s when he came to look at the job offer with the Heathman Hotel. Six years after Alice Waters opened Chez Panisse, another Bay Area resident opened a Pacific Northwest eatery in downtown McMinnville, Oregon. Nick Peirano and Nick's Italian Café never garner the culinary credentials that they deserve regarding Pacific Northwest cuisine. Nick and Alice had one other thing in common. Besides both being from the Bay Area, neither were trained chefs. For three decades, Nick Peirano was on top of his game. The meals I have consumed there have always represented some of the best Italian dishes on the planet. When Nick handed down the reins to his daughter Carmen and her husband, Eric, the restaurant never missed a beat. Nick's Italian Café is a dining destination requirement for anyone visiting the Pacific Northwest looking for the quintessential Willamette Valley food and wine experience.

Even in the city where James Beard, the monarch of American cuisine, originated, there was nothing like the concepts of cutting edge cuisine that would develop in the 1980s. The arrival of Greg Higgins in Portland and the diligent efforts of Jon Rowley in Puget Sound and beyond would change everything. The waves of culinary concepts just kept on rolling in. The success of Pacific Northwest wineries helped bring in new talent and new customers. Sometimes, the waves were too big, and there were some pretty nasty and expensive wipeouts. A few notable and extremely expensive crash and burns of consequence in the past few years were Troiani's in Seattle, opened by El Gaucho's parent company and a guy I used to work with in San Francisco, Rich Troiani. Ten 01 in Portland, opened by Jack Yoss, made some righteous food, and Erica Landon knew her wines. Doing sixty covers a night does not keep the doors open long with high-end food and excellent service. The most spectacular, reach-into-your-pockets deep wipeout has to be the three Dussin Group's upscale dining concepts Lucire, Fenouil and Blue Sage Café. The Dussin Group is the parent company to the Old Spaghetti Factory, a Portland concept created by Guss Dussin in 1969. I had some good meals at Fenouil, but none cooked by Chef Pascal Chureau. He was spread very thin while opening Lucire, the multimillion-dollar project that proved to be too upscale for Portland diners. N.W. Hayden Enterprises managed to divest investors of millions during the most tumultuous time for expansion in Portland's restaurant history.

The recession in the last decade created its own wave in the restaurant industry—a killer wave. Riding it out and surviving meant you had to be more than talented. You had to be creative, passionate, tough, talented and lucky, too. Making money serving people creative, high-quality food is brutal both physically and mentally. Putting your heart and soul into a restaurant that closes has sent many a chef off the deep end. I've known a few who found trying and failing cathartic and many more who eventually found a rehab center. Others find it inspirational, but that only happens after they find investors with money.

In Portland, a collaborative called ChefStable, a Kurt Huffman project, has revolutionized the entire concept of restaurant ownership. He is a hero to commercial restaurant property owners because he provides almost immediate reuse of former-restaurant spaces where the stoves have been turned off. Hoffman's understanding of real-time profit and loss (usually a weak spot with culinary talent) has enabled ChefStable to attract talent and investors. Kurt continues to move forward, fueling a frenzy of new restaurant openings. Kurt just recently found out if you open enough restaurants, eventually one will have to close. Two of his newest projects did not make it, but the great thing about ChefStable's system is that there is no need to hemorrhage for long or waste time on attempting to resuscitate. After just a few months, the group knew to pull the plug and walk away. The Pacific Northwest restaurant scene weathered the severe economic downturn of 2008 and 2009 better than a lot of places. That vacuum of dining dollars also served as a cleansing storm, eliminating a lot of outdated, mismanaged restaurant properties whose time had come.

The Portland vibe–style of dining (as the press likes to call it) has created enough buzz with its recognizably Pacific Northwest–innovative approach that many other cities are now duplicating the approach. The revival of restaurant expansion is rapidly growing here in Portland and Seattle with many chefs opening second and third locations, several in association with ChefStable. The following listing of restaurants is but a few of those very special people and places that make PDX and SEA a culinary destination. The 2013 James Beard Foundation Chef of the Year Western division winner, Gabriel Rucker, tops the list:

Gabriel Rucker: Le Pigeon and Little Bird
Vitaly and Kimberly Paley: Paley's Place, Imperial and Portland Penny Diner
John Gorham: Toro Bravo and Tasty and Sons
Toney Habetz: Bunk Sandwich and Trigger
Cathy Whims: Nostrana and Oven and Shaker
Ethan Stowell: Tavolata, How to Cook a Wolf, Anchovies & Olives, Staple & Fancy, Rione and XIII/Bar Cotto
Maria Hines: Tilth, Golden Beetle and Agrodolce
Matt Dillion: Sitka and Spruce, the Corson Building, Bar Sajor, Bar Ferdinand, Bread and the Old Chaser Farm

Just like most popular musicians, nobody on that list made it overnight. They've all cooked their hearts out, slinging food in hot, often unpleasant conditions and understanding that, ultimately, you are only as good as the last dish you made. Where do we go from here? Pacific Northwest food and wine have been thrust center stage to bask in the limelight as foodies and enophiles from all over the world clamor to get here to savor, taste and experience the dining revolution. For winemakers it is easy. Keep making the best natural wines the weather will allow, while letting the grapes express themselves without any undue manipulation. The culinary world is a different story. There might be a bit of uncertainty regarding where the current vanguard of indie kitchens wants to focus its efforts. It has come down to this: biodynamic, organic and locavore cuisine or circulation immersion sous vide and nitrogen-induced frozen tricks to the tongue. Can we have both? Of course, this is America, and you will always have a choice. Attempting to report on modern cuisine and have it still be relevant a decade from now is a pretty frivolous undertaking. I will, nevertheless, try.

Molecular Gastronomy

Before molecular gastronomy made its way to Spain and eventually to the Pacific Northwest, there were these two crazy guys—Nicholas Kurti, an Oxford physicist from Hungaria, and Hervé This. Hervé is a French physical chemist (think *Breaking Bad* but better) who started out attempting to test old-wives'-tales techniques in recipes. Hervé has cataloged some 25,000 assessments of culinary precisions (cooking techniques). These two wild and crazy guys coined the phrase molecular gastronomy in 1992 after presenting a series of workshops titled "Molecular and Physical Gastronomy."

For a second time in history, television would facilitate a cultural phenomenon in food culture when molecular gastronomy was first thrust into homes through a London television broadcast *Physicist in the Kitchen*, starring Nicholas Kurti, circa 1969. It was a lot like James Beard's early television appearances on *I Love to Eat* in 1946. For Kurti, using science in the kitchen was a unique presentation affording Londoners a look at modernist cuisine decades before modernist cuisine chefs could even spell sous-vide. Who knows if those early shows are still lurking around in the subconscious minds of chefs like Gordon Ramsey, Marco Pierre White or Heston Blumenthal.

It seems the phrase molecular gastronomy has already fallen out of favor and will be phased out. Replacing it will be the term *modern cuisine*. Pushing the limits of modern cuisine brought recognition to a place where nothing in food had changed for centuries. I find this somewhat ironic because they share a coastal border with both France and Italy, two countries that, throughout history, were known for their culinary dominance. I am referring to Spain, more specifically the Basque region, ground zero for molecular gastronomy—a blending of new technology, chemical engineering and cutting-edge culinary creativity. Ferran Adrià of El Bulli fame and Andoni Aduriz of Mugaritz have helmed those restaurants into worldwide recognition, both obtaining several Michelin stars and a line of talented chefs seeking an opportunity to apprentice there just to glimpse the culinary genius of these two masters.

Here in the Pacific Northwest, Matt Lightner, formerly of Castagna (now at New York City's Atera), was leading the charge for molecular gastronomy in the Pacific Northwest with his modernist cuisine before opting to cook for New Yorkers. Justin Woodward took over at Castagna, bringing with him his experience working with Chef Aduriz from Mugaritz in Errenteria, Spain. (Chef Lightner also trained with Aduriz, as well as at WD-50 in New York City.) Chef Woodward has been wowing guests at Castagna since taking over the restaurant from Matthew Lightner. Chef Rucker at Le Pigeon dabbles here and there with good results, but he does not need the modernist technique as a crutch. Gabriel's flavor and texture combinations pull together the ingredients he chooses for each dish in a natural procession seldom achieved consistently anywhere else.

In Seattle, Chef Jason Franey helms the kitchen at Canlis, a sixty-year old restaurant that brings the visual allure to the table and still has the best view in the Puget Sound. But walking the line between what the baby boomer regulars will accept and trying to create twenty-first-century cuisine that will appeal to a younger crowd has become a tightrope-balancing act.

Recently, the world's culinary eyes were forced to look away from the chefs in Northern Spain and focus on the Pacific Northwest, specifically Nathan Myhrvold, former chief technology officer for Microsoft. Nathan turned the culinary apple cart upside-down with the release of his *Modernist Cuisine: The Art and Science of Cooking* with coauthors Chris Young and Maxime Bilet in 2011. Often referred to as an amateur chef, Myhrvold has competed and won at Memphis in May, the world championship of barbeque contests. The precise manner of listing equipment, techniques and ingredients while guiding his readers through myriad technical steps that most culinarians have never attempted is anything but amateur. In perspective to his accomplishments as CTO at Microsoft, I am sure it is a walk in the park. Selling more than fifty thousand copies at a price of $625 astounded the literary world as much as it did the culinary world. The huge success of this book prompted the follow-up *Modernist Cuisine at Home*, and at a mere $140, it's a bargain. Both books cover cooking methods from microwave to sous-vide, as well as liquid nitrogen techniques, in detail.

In simple terms, Mr. Myhrvold talks about the sous-vide method:

> *Cooking sous vide is easier than its fancy name might suggest. You simply seal the ingredients in a plastic bag (you can also use a canning jar) and place them in a water bath, a combi oven, or any other cooker that can set and hold a target temperature to within a degree or two. When the food reaches your target temperature or time, you take it out, give it a quick sear or other finish, and serve it. That's it. The sous vide method yields results that are nearly impossible to achieve by traditional means.*

Johnny Zhu, who is the development chef for the cooking lab at Modernist Cuisine, talks about the microwave cooking method:

> *Max asked me one day whether I had any recipes for microwaved meat. It was a surprising question. In general, meat is awful in the microwave,*

no matter how you cook it. Our recipe in MC for microwaved jerky works around a common problem of microwave cooking—its tendency to dry out meat—by turning it into a useful technique. But when I started thinking about the question, I remembered that my mom was always telling me about this six-minute microwaved tilapia recipe, which mimics a traditional Chinese steamed fish dish. When I finally tried it, I remember thinking: wow, it's just as good as in a restaurant. It's tender, moist—not dry or chewy at all. So I pulled the recipe together for Max, and it turned out to be wonderful for what he wanted. As soon as I got my mom a copy of Modernist Cuisine, *I flipped right to that page and showed her the recipe, where it says "Adapted from Mrs. Zhu." She just beamed.*

The nice folks at the cooking lab (Nathan and the crew) very graciously agreed to let us reprint one of their recipes, and I chose my favorite. The following recipe for crispy chicken wings, Korean style, is more Pacific Northwest than one might think. The Korean fried chicken craze is all the rage in the Pacific Northwest. Boke Bowl here in Portland rakes in fifty dollars per Korean fried chicken and in Seattle, Ma'ono will sell you a whole bird for only thirty-nine.

CRISPY CHICKEN WINGS, KOREAN-STYLE

YIELD:	*four servings (1 kg / 20–24 pieces)*
TIME ESTIMATE:	*1 hour overall, including 30 minutes of preparation and 30 minutes unattended*
STORAGE NOTES:	*marinate, refrigerated, for up to one day before cooking*
LEVEL OF DIFFICULTY:	*easy*
SPECIAL REQUIREMENTS:	*michiu rice wine, Wondra, potato starch, monosodium glutamate (MSG, optional), Korean Wing Sauce (see below)*

This adaptation pairs Chinese-style velveting with Korean-style marinade and sauce. During frying, the starchy coating forms a barrier against moisture that allows the wing meat to remain juicy while the skin browns to a crisp. After many tests, we found that this combination of potato starch and Wondra, a prehydrated flour, crisped and browned the best. We also got good, crunchy results when breading the wings with other starches, such as corn, tapioca, and water chestnut starches. The *michiu* rice wine has a low boiling point, so it evaporates very quickly during frying and produces a very delicate crust. If *michiu* wine is unavailable, use sake, dry white wine, or three parts water to one part vodka instead.

INGREDIENT	WEIGHT	VOLUME	SCALING	PROCEDURE
Peanut oil	100 g	110 mL / ½ cup	10%	① Combine, and stir until the salt and sugar are completely dissolved to make a marinade.
Michiu rice wine (light)	70 g	80 mL / ⅓ cup	7%	
Soy sauce	20 g	15 mL / 3½ tsp	2%	
Salt	5 g	1¼ tsp	0.5%	
Toasted-sesame oil	5 g	5 mL / 1 tsp	0.5%	
Monosodium glutamate (MSG), optional	3 g		0.3%	
Sugar	2 g	½ tsp	0.2%	
Chicken wings, cut up	1 kg / 2.2 lb	20–24 pieces	100%	② Toss with the marinade, cover, and refrigerate for 30 minutes.
Neutral frying oil	as needed			③ Pour into a deep pot to no more than half full, and then preheat to 176 °C / 350 °F.
Wondra	40 g	¼ cup	4%	④ Combine.
Potato starch	38 g	¼ cup	3.8%	⑤ Dust over the marinade-soaked chicken wings, and stir until the wings are evenly coated with a thin batter.
				⑥ Deep-fry five to seven wings at a time until cooked through and golden brown, about 7 minutes.
				⑦ Drain the wings on paper towels.
Korean Wing Sauce see below	280 g	1½ cups	28%	⑧ Drizzle sauce generously over the wings, and toss to coat. Serve them hot.

KOREAN WING SAUCE

YIELD:	*280 g / 1 cup*
TIME ESTIMATE:	*15 minutes*
STORAGE NOTES:	*keeps for 5 days when refrigerated*
LEVEL OF DIFFICULTY:	*easy*
SPECIAL REQUIREMENTS:	*gochujang (Korean fermented chili paste), Shaoxing wine*

This sweet and spicy sauce is addictive. It is well worth the time to search your local Asian market for these specialty ingredients. Often sold in tubs, *gochujang* is a sweet, complex chili paste that you might find yourself slathering on almost everything. Look also for "thin mouth" (*usu kuchi*) soy sauce, the variety we prefer for this recipe. If you can't find Shaoxing wine (a Chinese rice wine), substitute medium-dry sherry.

INGREDIENT	WEIGHT	VOLUME	SCALING	PROCEDURE
Gochujang (Korean fermented chili paste)	135 g	½ cup	100%	① Combine, and whisk together until the sugar dissolves.
Sugar	50 g	⅓ cup	37%	② Serve the sauce warm or cold.
Soy sauce	30 g	25 mL / 5 tsp	22%	
Shaoxing wine	27 g	30 mL / 2 Tbsp	20%	
Toasted-sesame oil	20 g	20 mL / 1½ Tbsp	15%	
Garlic, minced	10 g	1 Tbsp	7.4%	
Ginger, minced	8 g	1 Tbsp	6%	

TIPS AND SUBSTITUTIONS

For Prepping the Wings:

You can find both michiu rice wine and monosodium glutamate (MSG) at Asian grocery stores.

MSG, which adds a savory flavor called umami, is the salt of glutamic acid. It is an amino acid, and thus it is found in many foods, such as parmesan cheese.

No scientific studies have linked MSG with health problems, but some people feel like they have a negative reaction to it. Feel free to leave it out.

If you can't find michiu wine, you can substitute sake, dry white wine or a mixture of three parts water to one part vodka.

Wondra flour can be found at any grocery store in the United States. If you live outside the United States, we recommend ordering it online.

For Deep-Frying the Wings:

Warm the wings to room temperature before frying.

If you have a deep fryer, you can use that instead of a pot on the stove.

The frying temperature in this recipe is slightly lower than some of our other chicken wing recipes because the Korean-style marinade is higher in sugar, and we want to avoid over-browning the batter.

Make sure you have an accurate thermometer to monitor the temperature of the oil.

It will take roughly seven minutes for the wings to cook in the oil. This may change, however, depending on the size of your pot or fryer. The more oil there is in the pot, the less it cools when the cold wings enter it and so the shorter the cooking time.

Cook in small batches to help minimize the cooling that occurs when you add the wings.

Fill the pot no more than half full in order to avoid spillovers. That being said, make sure you also use enough oil that the wings float and do not touch the sides of the pan. A large, deep pan is best.

Don't get too close to the oil. Use tongs, a slotted deep-frying spoon or a frying basket to insert and remove the wings.

Never use water, flour or sugar to put out a grease fire. And do not try to carry a flaming pot outdoors. Use baking soda, a damp towel or a fire extinguisher specifically designed for grease fires to suffocate the fire.

Drain the wings on paper towels to remove excess fat.

For the Korean Wing Sauce:

You can find gochujang (fermented chili paste) and Shaoxing wine (Chinese rice wine) at Asian grocery stores.

If you cannot find Shaoxing wine, you can substitute medium-dry sherry. Do not substitute mirrin as it is too sweet.

Whisk the ingredients together until the sugar has completely dissolved.

You can serve the sauce hot or cold. If you are coating the wings with the sauce, it is best to heat the sauce to room temperature.

Where are we heading with food preparation and consumption in the Pacific Northwest? Is molecular gastronomy becoming the new efficient way to prepare modern food by modern cooks in the modern home? Or will consumers want to ratchet up their health-conscious acumen and throw down with getting raw?

Organic and biodynamic-certified products will certainly become the new standard for ingredient quality. It's elementary—no really, just ask any third grader. Raw food/live food as mainstream dietary concepts are certainly gaining ground. Here in the Pacific Northwest, there are always raw/live food purveyors at farmers markets, probably because they know that is where the customer will go when they are out of product. Live food restaurants have been around for a while. Chef Juliano Brotman opened Raw in 1994 and trained the chef for actor Woody Harrelson's 02 Bar in West Hollywood, a raw/vegan oxygen bar opened in 1999. Most organic markets will have a range of premade products like hummus wraps and kale chips. House of the Sun brand is my personal favorite for kale chips. They come in many flavors, but I think the coconut-curry are the best. Raw foodism—whether it is in the form of raw vegan, raw vegetarian or raw omnivore diet—consists of primarily unheated food, or food cooked at less than 104 to 110 degrees Fahrenheit. It can be sun heated, cured or fermented too. It is possible to make tasty food in this concept, but you have to be crafty. Manipulating textures and flavor with the limited temperatures and methods of altering the base ingredients can be challenging. The main objective to obtain the benefits of this nutritional regimen is not to alter the product to a degree where it would diminish nutritional value. Ann Wigmore is credited with the development of noncooked foods as a homeopathic means to a healthier body and, by association, a healthier life. Physicians are leery of the movement, citing the adverse and possibly dangerous effects of eschewing traditional medicine while attempting to cure oneself of a serious disease through diet alone. Nevertheless, some advocates of the raw food movement claim the elimination of diabetes through maintaining a raw food diet. Supporters of the raw food lifestyle point to the natural enzymes that are lost when food is cooked, rendering the food useless as fuel to rebuild the body as the primary benefit. Some may argue those enzymes aid in achieving an optimum alkaline-acid balance in your body. Skeptics point out that enzymes, as with other proteins, are denatured and lysed in the digestive process after consumption, rendering them essentially noneffective. One thing is for certain: if you choose to adhere to a raw/live food regimen, you will lose weight. Results will vary, and it is advisable to consult a physician before trekking off down that path. Questioning how you choose to fuel your body is the starting point to a new and better way of life. You and only you are responsible for the performance of this machine you call your body, and remember when ingesting fuel that this machine carries your mind around also. Try to keep that in mind in the morning when your feet hit the floor, and oh yeah, decide to make good choices.

Realization is a good thing, especially when you realize it is time to explore. Deciding to explore our western borders beyond California to the north will expose you to a place where they do things differently and the grass is always greener. Our water is cleaner, the soil has several centuries less use than anything on the East Coast and our air is definitely fresher. Come explore the Pacific Northwest and enjoy the bounty this part of the country has to offer. Until then, savor the flavors of this unique region by preparing the following dishes: Macdaddy Marc's Dungeness crab cakes as an appetizer and Vitaly Paley's braised elk shoulder with mushrooms and cabbage for a full-flavored autumn one-pot main dish. I highly recommend buying the Paley's Place cookbook and visiting Paley's Place in Portland. A better representation of Pacific Northwest recipes would be hard to find anywhere. Vitaly and Kimberly are two of the best hospitalitarians in the business, and their restaurants have a natural flow of casual elegance that makes everyone feel welcome. Made from products indigenous to the Pacific Northwest, the following recipes highlight the wondrous bounty found from this region.

Macdaddy Marc's Dungeness Crab Cakes with Roasted Red Pepper Aioli
Serves four as a main or eight as an appetizer.

Ingredients for the crab cakes:
1 medium-sized sweet onion, small dice
2 small bell peppers any color, small dice
½ cup Italian parsley, chopped
1 stalk celery, diced
2 tablespoons lemon juice
2 tablespoons Dijon mustard
1 cup heavy cream
¼ cup dry white wine
1 pound cleaned Dungeness crabmeat
Tabasco to taste
2 egg yolks
1½ cups Panko breadcrumbs, ½ cup for the mixture, 1 cup to
    coat finished cakes before cooking
Salt and pepper to taste

Directions for crab cakes:
1. Dice the onions, celery and the peppers. In a medium-hot sauté
pan, cook vegetables until translucent. Then deglaze with white wine.
In another saucepan, scald heavy cream; then add the cream to the

vegetables. Cook down until almost sec (dry). Place the vegetables and cream mixture in a bowl to cool.

2. Pick through the crab to remove any shells. Squeeze all the liquid from the crab. When working with crab, always work in a bowl set in a bowl of ice. Five minutes of prep without refrigeration will dramatically reduce the shelf life of the finished product, especially if you freeze it and cook later.

3. Combine the vegetable cream mixture with egg, crab, lemon juice, parsley, Tabasco and breadcrumbs. Form into 4-ounce balls (or 2-ounce for appetizer size). Place on a sheet with additional breadcrumbs to coat the balls. Chill for 30 minutes before cooking.

4. Heat the oven to 400 degrees. Heat the sauté pan to medium high. Add peanut or canola oil to the sauté pan. Sautee crab cakes on both sides until golden brown. Place on sheet pan and finish in the oven for five to seven minutes; then flip. Cook for five more minutes or until cooked through with an internal temperature of 180 degrees.

Ingredients for the roasted red pepper sauce:
1 red bell pepper (roasted, peeled, seeded and chopped)
1 cup mayonnaise or fresh aioli
½ teaspoon paprika
2 tablespoons lemon juice
2 tablespoons chopped parsley
Salt and pepper to taste

Directions for sauce:
1. Roast the pepper over a gas flame. Once completely roasted, place it in a bowl and cover with plastic wrap, making sure you seal it tight. The steam from the trapped hot pepper will loosen the skin.

2. Once the pepper is cool (about 10 minutes), gently peel the skin off the pepper. Do not rinse with water. Cut open the top to remove the seedpod.

3. Place the red pepper, mayo (or aioli), paprika, lemon juice, chopped parsley, salt and pepper into a small food processor and blend until smooth.

4. Serve crab cakes on a bed of salad greens. I prefer arugula, but most any lettuce will work. Use sauce at your own discretion.

We recommend a good Oregon Pinot gris, such as Ponzi, or a Pinot blanc from Youngberg Hill to pair with these crab cakes.

Here is Vitaly Paley's recipe for braised elk shoulder with mushrooms and cabbage:

Paley's Place Braised Elk Shoulder with Mushrooms and Cabbage

1 (750-milliliter) bottle of red wine, preferably Pinot noir
1 carrot, peeled and sliced into ½-inch rounds
1 onion, quartered
1 bay leaf
5 sprigs of thyme
1 tablespoon whole black peppercorns
2½ pounds elk shoulder, bone in
Kosher salt and freshly ground black pepper
3 tablespoons extra virgin olive oil
3 cups chicken stock
4 large shallots, halved
1 small (about 1½ pound) fresh pig's foot
8 ounces of chanterelle or other wild or cultivated mushrooms
¼ head (about 8 ounces) savoy cabbage, cored and sliced into
　　1-inch ribbons

To prepare the marinade, combine the wine, carrot, onion, bay leaf, thyme and peppercorns in a large container or pot. Submerge the elk shoulder into the mixture, cover and refrigerate for at least six hours or overnight.

Remove the shoulder from the marinade, pat it dry with paper towels and set aside. Strain the marinade into a 2-quart saucepan and discard the solids. Cook the marinade over medium-high heat until reduced by half, skimming often to remove scum, about 10 minutes. Preheat the oven to 350 degrees.

Season the meat generously with salt and pepper. In a large Dutch oven, heat the oil over high heat and sear the meat brown on both sides, *about four minutes per side. Remove the meat and set aside. Discard the cooking oil.*

Add the reduced marinade and stock to the Dutch oven and bring to a boil over high heat. Add the shoulder, shallots and pig's foot, cover tightly and place in oven.

Braise for 1 hour and then turn over the elk shoulder and pig's foot and add the mushrooms and cabbage. Cover again and continue to braise until elk is fork tender and the meat from the pig's foot is falling off the bone, about 1½ hours longer.

Remove from the oven. Transfer the pig's foot to a bowl and set aside until cool enough to handle. Everything but the bones is edible. Carefully pick the meat from the bones (of which there are many) and tear into bite-sized pieces.

Return the meat from the pig's foot to the Dutch oven and mix with the elk meat. On the stove, gently bring the mixture to a simmer over medium low heat. Season with salt and pepper if needed and serve, family style, in a large, deep platter.

A 2010 Tendril Tightrope Pinot noir would make a great wine pairing with this dish. It is a Willamette Valley wine sourced from two southern-facing hillside vineyards in the Yamhill-Carlton AVA. Tony Rynders (formerly of Domaine Serene) is now making his own wines and doing a great job of it. The Tightrope will pair perfectly with this rustic Pacific Northwest dish, bringing its red- and blue-fruit flavor profile and nuances of coffee, spice and earthy terroir to the table to make a match made in heaven. Preparing either of those two recipes will give you an idea of the state of culinary nirvana you can obtain and maintain if you live in the Pacific Northwest—seasonal, local, fresh, bountiful organic ingredients available year-round.

It has been a very long trip from Sequim, Washington, and the discovery of a fourteen-thousand-year-old mastodon to the current state of culinary affairs and the newest form of culinary technique, molecular gastronomy. If you already live in the Pacific Northwest, I hope you have gleaned some nuggets of information that help you realize you live in one of the best places in the world for food and wine. If you do not live here, eat as many Washington apples, Oregon hazelnuts, Columbia River salmon and Pacific Dungeness crabs as you can find, while drinking as much Pacific Northwest wine as you can get. Come see us when you can, and always remember to eat well, drink well and live well.

Bibliography

Listed here are the works that I have used directly in the making of this book. By no means does it represent a holistic record of works consulted. It simply indicates the substance and extent of material gathered for me to formulate ideas while pulling together the breadth of the Pacific Northwest food and wine scene. I rely mainly on the conversations and interviews I have had throughout the years with winemakers, vintners, chefs and wine industry professionals to build a thorough and complete history that makes this book what it is.

Becker, Paula. "Prohibition in Washington State." HistoryLink.org. November 20, 2010. http://www.historylink.org/index.cfm?DisplayPage=output.cfm&file_id=9630 (accessed April 17, 2013).

———. "Schanno Family Plants the First Wine Grapes in the Yakima Valley Near Union Gap in 1869." HistoryLink.org. http://www.historylink.org/index.cfm?DisplayPage=output.cfm&file_id=5275 (accessed January 15, 2013).

Berger, Dan. "Winemaking "Rebels" Quieting Critics." *Oregonian*, July 2, 1976: 35.

Bonné, Jon. "Livermore Wine History's Powerful Start." *SF Gate*, March 1, 2013. http://www.sfgate.com/wine/article/Livermore-wine-history-s-powerful-start-4321615.php#ixzz2UXOoU1u6 (accessed March 2, 2013).

Cancler, Carole, "The Interesting Tribal Lore Surrounding the Makah Ozette Potato." *Examiner.com.* http://www.examiner.com/farmers-market-in-seattle/the-interesting-tribal-lore-surrounding-the-makah-ozette-potato (accessed May 23, 2010).

Chalmers, W. "Yamhill County Winemaking Comes of Age." *Oregonian*, October 12, 1972: 18.

Chapel, I.G. *An All-Western Conservation Cook Book*. Portland, OR: Modern Printing & Publishing Co., 1917.

Coleman, Patrick Alan. "Greg Higgins: Extended Interview." *Portland Mercury*, July 24, 2008. http://www.portlandmercury.com/BlogtownPDX/archives/2008/07/24/greg-higgins-extended-intervi (accessed May 12, 2013).

Corlett, R.T.. "Megafaunal Extinctions in Tropical Asia." *Tropinet* 17, no. 3 (2006): 1–3.

Cushman, H.B. *History of the Choctaw, Chickasaw and Natchez Indians.* Greenville, TX: Headlight Printing House, 1899.

Daily Morning Astorian. "Electric Liquor." June 5, 1885. http://oregonnews.uoregon.edu/lccn/sn96061150/1885-06-05/ed-1/seq-1/ (accessed January 22, 2013).

Davidis, Henriette. *Practical Cookbook for the Ordinary and Elegant Kitchen.* 23rd edition. Bielefeld and Leipzig, Germany: Velhagen & Klasing, 1879.

Domine, Andre. *Wine.* Potsdam, Germany: Ullmann Publishing, 2008: 798–800.

Edmeades, Baz. *Megafauna: First Victims of the Human-Caused Extinction.* http://megafauna.com/table-of-contents/ (Accessed October 4, 2010).

Erdoes, Richard. *Saloons of the Old West.* New York: Alfred A. Knopf, 1979: 110–14.

Fagundes, Nelson J.R., et al.. "Mitochondrial Population Genomics Supports a Single Pre-Clovis Origin with a Coastal Route for the Peopling of the Americas." *American Journal of Human Genetics* 82, no. 3 (2008): 583–92.

"The Food Journal of Lewis & Clark: Recipes for an Expedition," Palaeontologia Electronica. http://palaeo-electronica.org/2006_1/books/food.pdf (accessed January 7, 2012).

Gernet, J. *Daily Life in China on the Eve of the Mongol Invasion, 1250–1276.* Translated by H.M. Wright. Stanford, CA: Stanford University Press, 1962.

Goebel, T., M.R. Waters and D.H. O'Rourke. "The Late Pleistocene Dispersal of Modern Humans in the Americas." *Science*, March 14, 2008: 319 (5869), 1497–1502.

"Grapes Can Be Grown in Oregon." *Willamette Farmer* (1872). http://oregonnews.uoregon.edu/lccn/sn85042522/1872-10-19/ed-1/seq-3/ (accessed July 24, 2012).

Green, Frank S. *Ezra Meeker—Pioneer: A Guide to the Ezra Meeker Papers in the Library of the Washington State Historical Society.* Tacoma: Washington State Historical Society, 1969.

Green, V., and K. Wallig. "African Americans in Salem." Salem Online History. http://www.salemhistory.net/people/african_americans.htm (accessed March 28, 2013).

Hastings, Lansford W. "The Equipment, Supplies, and the Method of Traveling." Chap. 15 in *The Emigrants' Guide to Oregon and California.* Cincinnati, OH: George Conclin, 1815. Available online from the University of Virginia. http://xroads.virginia.edu/~HYPER/IGUIDE/or-ch15.htm (accessed July 14, 2010).

Henninger, Jean. "Oregon's Future Fertile for Fine Wines." *Oregonian*, September 11, 1968: 30.

Hodgen, Donald A. "U.S. Wine Industry—2011." U.S. Department of Commerce. http://ita.doc.gov/td/ocg/wine2011.pdf (accessed June 17, 2013).

Hood, Michael. "Rosellini, Victor (1915–2003), Restaurateur and Epicure." HistoryLink.org, July 26, 2002. http://www.historylink.org/index.cfm?DisplayPage=output.cfm&file_id=3902 (accessed May 17, 2013).

"Hudson's Bay Company." http://www.hbcheritage.ca/hbcheritage/home (accessed March 14, 2012).

Huelsbeck, David R. "Whaling in the Precontact Economy of the Central Northwest Coast." *Arctic Anthropology* 25, no. 1 (1988): 1–15 http://www.jstor.org/stable/40316151 (accessed June 2, 2010).

Hunt, Robert R. "Ardent Spirits on the Expedition." *Discovering Lewis & Clark.* http://lewis-clark.org/content/content-article.asp?ArticleID=2505 (accessed July 19, 2010).

Irvine, Ronald, Clore Irvine and Walter J. *The Wine Project: Washington State's Winemaking History.* Vashone, WA: Sketch Publications, 1997.

Johansen, Dorothy O. *Empire of the Columbia: A History of the Pacific Northwest.* 2nd ed. New York: HarperCollins, 1967.

"The Journals of the Lewis and Clark Expedition." Journals. http://lewisandclarkjournals.unl.edu/read/?_xmlsrc=lc.toc.xml&_xslsrc=LCstyles.xsl (accessed December 2, 2011).

Judson, Katharine Berry. *Legends of the Pacific Northwest: Especially of Washington and Oregon.* Chicago: A.C. McClurg, 1910.

Kristiansen, T.M. and H. Batey. *New Royal Cookbook.* New York: Royal Baking Powder Co, 1920. Available online from Project Gutenberg. www.gutenberg.org/files/38193/38193-h/38193-h.htm (accessed August 19, 2010).

Lamy, Jeffrey L. "Bill Fuller, Oregon Wine Pioneer." Enobytes Wine Online. http://enobytes.com/2013/03/05/bill-fuller-wine-pioneer/ (accessed April 5, 2013).

Lang, Herbert O., ed. *History of the Willamette Valley: Being a Description of the Valley and Its Resources....*Portland, OR: Himes & Lang, 1885. Available online as Google e-book. http://books.google.ca/books?id=C9QtAAAAYAAJ (accessed May 17, 2010).

Larsen, Dennis M. *The Missing Chapters: The Untold Story of Ezra Meeker's Old Oregon Trail Monument Expedition January 1906 to July 1908.* Puyallup, WA: Ezra Meeker Historical Society, 2006.

Lasley, Paul, and Elizabeth Harryman. "Portland Has a Lot More Than Bread and Beer." *Los Angeles Times.* http://articles.latimes.com/1989-10-22/travel/tr-648_1_beer-bread (accessed January 22, 2013).

Lawrence, N. "Wineries Find Oregon Climate, Soil Fine for Wine." *Oregonian,* November 7, 1978: 23.

Lebaron, Gaye. "Turns Out That Homemade Wine in Prohibition Wasn't Legal," *Press Democrat.* http://www.napavalley.edu/people/gvierra/Documents/Fundamentals_of_Enology_Class/ProhibitionsLegality.pdf (accessed June 4, 2013).

"The Lewis & Clark Cookbook: Historic Recipes from the Corps of Discovery and Jefferson's American." Lewis & Clark Hunting on the Trail. http://lewisandclarktrail.com/hunting.htm (accessed July 19, 2012).

"The Louisiana Purchase Legislative Timeline." Library of Congress. http://memory.loc.gov/ammem/amlaw/louisiana1.html (accessed April 2, 2012).

Marcy, Randolph B. "The Prairie Traveler." *Kansas Collection Books.* http://www.kancoll.org/books/marcy/machap01.htm (accessed March 2, 2012).

McLagan, Elizabeth. "A Very Prejudiced State: Discrimination in Oregon, 1900–1940." Chap. 8 in *A Peculiar Paradise: A History of Blacks in Oregon, 1788–1940.* http://gesswhoto.com/paradise-chapter8.html (accessed November 14, 2012).

Mead, Jim I. "Mammoth Trumpet: Linking Two America's." *University of Maine.* Newsletter 3 (1987): 2–5. http://csfa.tamu.edu/mammoth/issues/Volume-03/vol3_num3.pdf (accessed January 7, 2010).

Morgan, Dale L. *Jedediah Smith and the Opening of the American West.* Lincoln, London: University of Nebraska Books, 1953, 1964.

Morning Oregonian. "Beer Sure Friday Under Riley's Plan: 400 Apply for Licenses." April 4, 1933: 12.

Newberg Graphic Farm News. "Purchase Old Blanchard Place." February 16, 1967.

"Nez Perce (Nee-Me-Poo) National Historic Trail, Traditional Foods and Recipes." United States Department of Agriculture. http://www.fs.usda.gov/detail/npnht/learningcenter/history-culture/?cid=stelprdb5312571 (accessed July 24, 2012).

Noles, B.J. "Grape Grower's Success Proves Thesis." *Oregonian,* August 13, 1972: 38.

Oregon Blue Book. "Oregon History: Emerging Economies, 1859–Present." http://www.bellevuereporter.com/community/19195374.html (accessed January 12, 2012).

Oregon Encyclopedia. S.v., "Community of Verboort." http://www.oregonencyclopedia.org/entry/view/verboort_community_/ (accessed February 23, 2013).

———. S.v., "Woman Suffrage in Oregon." http://www.oregonencyclopedia.org/entry/view/woman_suffrage_in_oregon/ (accessed April 1, 2013).

Oregonian. "Grape Crop All Sold." October 21, 1934: 42.

"Oregon's First Brewer: Henry Saxer." Saxer Oregon Lagers. http://www.saxerbeer.com/ (accessed May 7, 2013).

Pappas, Stephanie. "Ancient Seafood Buffet Uncovered on Channel Islands." Live Science. http://www.livescience.com/13066-channel-island-seafood-buffet-uncovered.html (accessed June 7, 2011).

Peterson-Nedry, J. "Wineries in Oregon Uncork Potential." *Oregonian,* June 18, 1981: E1.

Pinney, Thomas. *A History of Wine in America: From Prohibition to the Present.* Volume 2. Berkeley: University of California Press, 2007.

Polino, Valerie Ann. "Early Man in North America: The Known to the Unknown." *Yale-New Haven Teachers Institute.* http://www.yale.edu/ynhti/curriculum/units/1980/2/80.02.07.x.html (accessed January 12, 2011).

Pomeroy, Earl. *The Pacific Slope: A History.* Reno: University of Nevada, 1965.

Radhuber, S.G. "A Look at What Goes into Oregon's Fruit Wines." *Northwest,* January 15, 1978: 6.

Richards, Seth. *A Narrative of the Adventures and Sufferings of John R. Jewitt, Only Survivor of the Crew of the Ship Boston....*Middletown, CT: 1815. Available online from Google books. http://books.google.com/books?id=HCETAAAAYAAJ&printsec=frontcover#v=onepage&q&f=false (accessed December 12, 2010).

Riley, Carroll L. "The Makah Indians: A Study of Political and Economic Organization." *Ethnohistory* 15, no. 1 (Winter 1968): 57–95 http://www.jstor.org/stable/480818 (accessed March 28, 2011).

Robbins, William G. *Landscapes of Promise: The Oregon Story, 1800–1940.* Seattle: University of Washington Press, 1997.

———. *Oregon, This Storied Land.* Portland: Oregon Historical Society, 2005.

Robinson, Jancis. *The Oxford Companion to Wine.* 3rd edition. Oxford, UK: Oxford University Press, 2006.

Rojas-Burke, J. "Discovery by Oregon Archaeologist Looks 12,000 Years into Past at People Who Settled the West Coast." *Oregonian.* http://www.oregonlive.

com/environment/index.ssf/2011/03/discovery_by_oregon_archaeolog.html (accessed August 2, 2010).

Rothert, Y. "Wine Expert Lauds Oregon's Infant Vineyards." *Oregonian*, September 6, 1973: 40.

Rowley, Jon, "The Beautiful Taste." http://jonrowley.com/ (accessed June 28, 2013).

Schneider, John. "The Beginnings of KJR." Seattle Radio History. 2011. http://www.theradiohistorian.org/Seattle/kjr%20komo%20history.htm (accessed February 19, 2013).

Schneider, Wendie Ellen. "Past Imperfect: Irving v. Penguin Books Ltd., No. 1996-I-1113, 2000 WL 362478 (Q. B. Apr. 11), appeal denied (Dec. 18, 2000)." *Yale Law Journal* 110, no. 8 (June 2001): 1531–45.

Sepez, Jennifer. "Historical Ecology of Makah Subsistence Foraging Patterns." *Journal of Ethnobiology* 28, no. 1: 110–33 (2008). doi: http://dx.doi.org/10.2993/0278-0771(2008)28[110:HEOMSF]2.0.CO;2, (accessed June 11, 2011).

"Sex, Dog Meat, and the Lash: Odd Facts About Lewis and Clark." *National Geographic News.* http://news.nationalgeographic.com/news/2003/12/1204_031204_lewisclark.html (accessed March 12, 2012).

Smith, F.A., S.M. Elliot and S.K. Lyons. "Methane Emissions from Extinct Megafauna." *Nature Geoscience* 3, no. 6 (May 23, 2010): 374–5. http://www.nature.com/ngeo/journal/v3/n6/full/ngeo877.html (accessed May 12, 2012).

Sunday Oregonian. "Making of Wine in the Chehalem Hills of Oregon." October 30, 1904. Accessed March 2, 2013.

———. "World's Greatest Recipes for the Food We Send Abroad: Sweet Potato and Prune Zimes." July 7, 1946: 8.

Thoms, Dr. Alston. "First American Roots—Literally." The Mammoth Trumpet, April, 2007.

"Von Pessel Sells Winery." *(Roseburg, OR) Plaindealer*, October 15, 1903. Accessed March 2, 2013.

"Washington Wineries, Wines and Wine Country." Wines Northwest. http://www.winesnw.com/wahome.html (accessed February 4, 2013).

Waters, Michael R., Thomas W. Stafford Jr., Gregory H. McDonald, Carl Gustafson, Morten Rasmussen, Enrico Cappellini, Jesper V. Olsen, et al. "Pre-Clovis Mastodon Hunting 13,800 Years Ago at the Manis Site, Washington." *Science* 334, no. 6054: 351–3 (accessed January 12, 2012).

West, Stephen H. "Playing with Food: Performance, Food, and the Aesthetics of Artificiality in the Sung and Yuan." *Harvard Journal of Asiatic Studies* 57, no. 1 (1997): 67–106.

Wikipedia. S.v. "Alexander Mackenzie (explorer)." http://en.wikipedia.org/wiki/Alexander_Mackenzie_%28explorer%29 (last modified August 30, 2012).

———. S.v., "Edmond-Charles Genêt." http://en.wikipedia.org/wiki/Edmond-Charles_Gen%C3%AAt (last modified July 31, 2012).

———. S.v., "John Jacob Astor." http://en.wikipedia.org/wiki/John_Jacob_Astor (last modified April 06, 2013).

———. S.v., "Otokichi," http://en.wikipedia.org/wiki/Otokichi (last modified August 6, 2012).

————. S.v., "Paisley Caves," http://en.wikipedia.org/wiki/Paisley_Caves (last modified July 17, 2012).

————. S.v., "Portable Soup." http://en.wikipedia.org/wiki/Portable_soup (last modified July 7, 2012).

————. S.v., "Robert Gray's Columbia River expedition." http://en.wikipedia.org/wiki/Robert_Gray%27s_Columbia_River_expedition (last modified July 3, 2012).

————. S.v., "Treaty of 1818. http://en.wikipedia.org/wiki/Anglo-American_Convention_of_1818 (last modified August 11, 2012).

————.S.v.,"War of 1812." http://en.wikipedia.org/wiki/War_of_1812#Impressment (last modified April 05, 2013).

PERSONAL INTERVIEWS WITH THE AUTHORS

DeMara, Dyson. Interview by Marc Hinton and Pamela Heiligenthal. Roseburg, OR. March 30, 2012.

Engeman, Richard H. Interview by Marc Hinton and Pamela Heiligenthal. Portland, OR. March 27, 2012.

Gallick, Paul. Interview by Marc Hinton and Pamela Heiligenthal. Honeywood Winery, Salem, OR. March 24, 2012.

Shea, Dick and Deirdre. Interview by Marc Hinton and Pamela Heiligenthal. Shea Vineyards, Newberg, OR. April 6, 2012.

Index

Disclaimer

As I was struggling to write this book—looking at all the information from a historically objective point of view while attempting to weave the episodes, stories and scenarios about the gradual evolution of the Pacific Northwest's food and drink culture into one of the hottest culinary scenes in the world into a narrative almost anyone in a somewhat sober state of mind could follow—the need for a code to use for conducting my research became apparent. In my search for what an objective historian does, I ran across this list. It is a very good code for writing a book about historical events, and as best I could, I maintained a strict intention to abide by all seven covenants of the code published by Wendy E. Schneider in the *Yale Law Journal:*

> *1. The historian must treat sources with appropriate reservations;*
> *2. The historian must not dismiss counterevidence without scholarly consideration;*
> *3. The historian must be even-handed in treatment of evidence and eschew "cherry-picking";*
> *4. The historian must clearly indicate any speculation;*
> *5. The historian must not mistranslate documents or mislead by omitting parts of documents;*
> *6. The historian must weigh the authenticity of all accounts, not merely those that contradict a favored view; and*
> *7. The historian must take the motives of historical actors into consideration.*

The first rule is pretty easy to adhere to, because I do not trust anyone.

Number two is not applicable, because someone would have to read the book first to offer counterevidence.

Number three is very applicable for the Pacific Northwest, but it has been my experience that you have to be very evenhanded when you are cherry picking.

Number four I am glad to see because I would clearly like to indicate some speculation.

The fifth is quite appropriate, and should there be any discrepancies, it will become my favorite amendment.

For number six, as much as it might be the path of less resistance to accept history as it's written, on this one, I will defer to number one.

For number seven, I thought a lot about the players on this project, and I have to say that when it comes to motives, I've learned they're a lot like a sense of humor: everybody has one but it's not always good.

It's good to have a code.

About the Author

Committed to celebrating hospitality with pride, Marc Hinton is a freelance writer and editor-at-large for the online wine publication *Enobytes.com*. He has over thirty years of experience in the food and wine industry. Beginning his culinary journey in Memphis as a dishwasher drinking straw-basket Chianti, he has worked as an executive chef in Boston, Chicago and San Francisco, where he switched to working at wineries and distributors in sales and marketing for both retail and wholesale environments. Now residing in the Northwest, Marc provides restaurant consulting, cooking classes and wine-education classes. He is a wine contributor to *OregonLive.com* with his unique and engaging *Wine Bytes* column and has appeared on Portland's *Vine Time* on News Radio 750 KXL and on California's Central Coast *From the Growing of the Grape to the Glass* on KUHL-AM 1410.

Visit us at
www.historypress.net
....
This title is also available as an e-book